W9-BCQ-708

Life's Tough Questions

What The Bible Says About.....

- Suffering
- Depression
- Demon Possession
- Abortion
- Suicide
- Pastoral Care and Death Issues
- Mental Illness

Dr. Steven Waterhouse
Th.M., D.Min.

Westcliff Press
P.O. Box 1521, Amarillo TX 79105

Suggested Cataloging-in-Publication Data

Waterhouse, Steven W.
Life's Tough Questions
207p. 21.6cm.
Includes Biblical References
ISBN 0-9702418-6-0
1. Pastoral Counseling 2. Depression, Mental – Religious
Aspects 3. Suffering - Religious Aspects 4. Abortion – Religious
Aspects 5. Bereavement – Religious Aspects 6. Pastoral
Theology.
Suggested Library of Congress Number BV4012.2
Suggested Dewey Number 253.5

About The Author

Dr. Steven Waterhouse has served as the Pastor of Westcliff Bible Church in Amarillo, Texas, since 1985. He has degrees from Dallas Theological Seminary (D.Min.); Capital Bible Seminary, Lanham MD (Th.M. in Hebrew and Greek); Spring Arbor University in Michigan (B.A. Social Science); and Cornerstone University in Grand Rapids, Michigan.

Information about this book and others written by Dr. Waterhouse can be accessed at his web site: **www.webtheology.com**

Other Titles By Steven Waterhouse

Not By Bread Alone; An Outlined Guide to Bible Doctrine

*Strength For His People; A Ministry For the
Families of the Mentally Ill*

Blessed Assurance; A Defense of the Doctrine of Eternal Security

*What Must I Do To Be Saved; The Bible's Definition of Saving
Faith*

(Available on amazon.com or at www.webtheology.com)

Westcliff Press
P.O. Box 1521
Amarillo TX 79105
1-806-359-6362
westcliff@amaonline.com
www.webtheology.com

ISBN: 0-9702418-6-0
Library of Congress Catalog Card Number 2004116500

Printed in the United States of America

Cover by Slawomir Konieczniak, Poland

Acknowledgment

The congregation of Westcliff Bible Church,
Amarillo, Texas deserves praise for allowing
pastoral energies to be devoted to
Bible study and for the
financial backing of Bible research.

Editor's Note

This book has been published to help. It is a compilation of Dr. Waterhouse's several papers written over time as an extension of his ministry to the families of the mentally ill. In his book, *Strength For His People*, Dr. Waterhouse, drawing upon his experience of growing up with a schizophrenic brother, provides Biblical counsel for families who find themselves faced with the devastating need to care for a family member who has been afflicted with mental illness. *Life's Tough Questions* extends this ministry into the areas of suffering, depression, the recognition of demon possession, suicide prevention, and counseling for those who must minister to people who have lost a loved one or may themselves be close to death. To these subjects have been added Dr. Waterhouse's thesis on the abortion issue, which looks at the sanctity of life viewed from the original Hebrew and Greek languages that mention the unborn.

Included is a work entitled "Square One Theology", written by E. Jay O'Keefe, a founding elder of Westcliff Bible Church. "Square One" is a fitting supplement to the counseling papers of Dr. Waterhouse, having at its foundation the undeniable fact that "God is in control and has my best interest at heart".

The defining characteristic of Dr. Waterhouse's writing is that whether Bible Doctrine or counseling, it is without exception based directly upon Scripture. The reader will find that for every paragraph within this text there is always supporting Biblical evidence, and may be assured that whatever the counsel, explanation, or application, it will never be based upon anything but God's Word.

The author and the congregation of Westcliff Bible Church commend to the reader their hope that "*Life's Tough Questions*" will provide blessing and help for those who are in need.

Alan N Good, Editor

Life's Tough Questions

What The Bible Says About.....

Dr. Steven Waterhouse

Table of Contents

SUFFERING;

WHAT GOOD IS IT?

Why doesn't God finish the devil and
end all suffering?

This study was prepared for
lectures at Capital Bible Seminary, Lanham, MD
and for pastoral care for those in pain.

SUFFERING;
WHAT GOOD IS IT?

Introduction

The Old Testament Book of Job illustrates that even if we do not know why God permits a given case of suffering, we know how to endure (Job 13:15). Job trusted God even when he did not understand following the pattern given in Proverbs 3:5,6: *"Trust in the Lord with all your heart, lean not to your own understanding. In all your ways acknowledge Him, and He will make your paths straight"*.

In helping others who suffer, it is best if counselors remain silent about mysterious aspects (Job 13:5). However, unlike Job's friends, counselors today have the complete Scriptures. We may not know all the secrets about God's ways (Isa. 55:8, 9), and caution is in order in categorically diagnosing God's purpose for another's hardships, but the Bible gives possible reasons and benefits for suffering. "Seeing in a mirror darkly" is an improvement over total darkness.

Many are the afflictions of the righteous, BUT...(Psa. 34:19).

Sixteen points suggest answers as to why God continues to allow suffering.

1. <u>Suffering destroys the illusion of self-sufficiency and keeps us totally dependent upon God.</u>

• **He humbled you** and let you be hungry, and fed you with manna which you did not know, nor did your fathers know, **that He might make you understand that man does not live**

by bread alone, but man lives by everything that proceeds out of the mouth of the Lord [Deut. 8:3].

• And because of the surpassing greatness of the revelations, for this reason, **to keep me from exalting myself**, there was given me a thorn in the flesh, a messenger of Satan to torment me - to keep me from exalting myself....And He has said to me, "My grace is sufficient for you, for power is perfected in weakness" [2 Cor. 12:7, 9].

• When I am afraid, I will put my trust in Thee [Psa. 56:3].

• Simon Peter answered Him, "Lord, to whom shall we go? You have words of eternal life" [John 6:68].

2. Suffering teaches us to pray.

• Now about that time Herod the king laid hands on some who belonged to the church, in order to mistreat them....So Peter was kept in the prison, but **prayer for him was being made fervently by the church to God** [Acts 12:1 and 5].

• And He went a little beyond them, and **fell on His face and prayed,** saying, "My Father, if it is possible, let this cup pass from Me; yet not as I will, but as Thou wilt" [Matt. 26:39].

3. Suffering causes us to study the Bible.

• It is good for me that I **was afflicted, that I may learn Thy statutes** [Psa. 119:71].

• My soul cleaves to the dust; **revive me according to Thy word**.... My soul weeps because of grief; **strengthen me according to Thy word** [Psa. 119:25 and 28].

4. Suffering makes us sympathetic and gives us credibility in ministry to others needs.

• ...the Father of mercies and God of all comfort; who comforts us in all our affliction so **that we may be able to comfort those who are in any affliction** with the comfort with which we ourselves are comforted by God [2 Cor. 1:3-4].

5. Suffering draws families and friends together.

• ...weep with those who weep [Rom. 12:15].

• That there may be no division in the body, but that the members may have the same care for one another. And if one member suffers, all the members suffer with it...1 Cor. 12: 25-26a].

6. Suffering corrects priorities causing us to distinguish the eternal from the transitory, the important from the non-essential.

• For momentary, light affliction is producing for us an eternal weight of glory far beyond all comparison, while we look not at the things which are seen, but at the things which are not seen; for the things which are seen are temporal, but the things which are not seen are eternal [2 Cor. 4:17-18].

• For all that is in the world, the lust of the flesh and the lust of the eyes and the boastful pride of life, is not from the Father, but is from the world. And the world is passing away, and also its lusts; but the one who does the will of God lives forever [1 John 2:16-17].

7. Suffering enables us to glorify God by increased witness to believers and unbelievers alike.

- Jesus answered, "It was neither that this man sinned, nor his parents; but it was **so that the works of God might be displayed in him**" [John 9:3].

- But when Jesus heard it, He said, "**This sickness** is not unto death, but **for the glory of God**, so that the Son of God may be glorified by it" [John 11:4].

- But the chief priests took counsel that they might put Lazarus to death also; because on account of him many of the Jews were going away, and were believing in Jesus [John 12:10-11].

8. <u>Suffering can lead to salvation for the afflicted or for others who would not listen to the gospel any other way.</u>

- And he was longing to fill his stomach with the pods that the swine were eating, and no one was giving anything to him. But **when he came to his senses....I will get up and go to my father** [Luke 15:16-18].

Personal suffering drives many to the decision to trust in the Lord Jesus Christ as Savior. He paid for our sins on the cross and rose again. He asks us to put our faith in Him as Savior.

Sometimes it is another person's suffering that causes one to realize his own spiritual need or to listen to the gospel message.

9. <u>Suffering deepens our understanding of God's character.</u>

- Take My yoke upon you and learn from Me...[Matt. 11:29].

10. <u>The chronic suffering of those with hardships teaches us the sanctity of human life.</u>

• The King will answer and say to them, "Truly I say to you, to the extent that you did it to one of these brothers of Mine, even the least of them, you did it to Me" [Matt. 25:40 (by application)]

11. <u>Suffering causes us a greater appreciation of blessings by contrast.</u>

• Bless the Lord, O my soul; and all that is within me, bless His holy name. Bless the Lord, O my soul, and **forget none of His benefits**; Who pardons all your iniquities; Who heals all your diseases; Who redeems your life from the pit...[Psa. 103:1-4a].

12. Suffering tests our loyalty and faith (we understand keeping a covenant).

• And the Lord said to Satan, "**Have you considered My servant Job? For there is no one like him on the earth, a blameless and upright man, fearing God and turning away from evil**". Then Satan answered the Lord, "Does Job fear God for nothing? Hast Thou not made a hedge about him and his house and all that he has, on every side? Thou hast blessed the work of his hands, and his possessions have increased in the land. But put forth Thy hand now and touch all that he has; he will surely curse Thee to Thy face." Then the Lord said to Satan, "Behold, all that he has is in your power, only do not put forth your hand on him". So Satan departed from the presence of the Lord [Job 1:8-12].

• Though He slay me, I will hope in Him [Job 13:15a].

• But He knows the way I take; when He has tried me, I shall come forth as gold [Job 23:10].

• [T]hat the proof of **your faith,** being more precious than gold which is perishable, even though **tested by fire, may be found to result in praise and glory and honor** at the revelation of Jesus Christ; and though you have not seen Him, you love Him, and though you do not see Him now, but believe in Him, you greatly rejoice with joy inexpressible and full of glory, obtaining as the outcome of your faith the salvation of your souls [1 Pet. 1:7-9].

13. <u>Suffering can correct our sins to bring us back to God.</u>

•...Behold, you have become well; **do not sin anymore, so that nothing worse may befall you** [John 5:14b].

•...**for those whom the Lord loves He disciplines**...It is for discipline that you endure; God deals with you as with sons; for what son is there whom his father does not discipline?...All discipline for the moment seems not to be joyful, but sorrowful; yet to those who have been trained by it, afterwards it yields the peaceful fruit of righteousness [Heb. 12:6a,7,11].

14. <u>Suffering causes us to appreciate God's strength and wisdom by contrast to our own limitations.</u>

• **Why do you say,** O Jacob, and assert, O Israel, **"My way is hidden from the Lord, and the justice due me escapes the notice of my God"?** Do you not know? Have you not heard? The everlasting God, the Lord, the Creator of the ends of the earth does not become weary or tired. His understanding is inscrutable. **He gives strength to the weary, and to him who lacks might He increases power.** Though youths grow weary and tired, and vigorous young men stumble badly, yet those who wait for the Lord will gain new strength; they will mount up with wings like eagles, they will run and not get tired, they will walk and not become weary [Isa. 40:27-31].

15. Suffering creates greater endurance.

• Consider it all joy, my brethren, when you encounter various trials; knowing that **the testing of your faith produces endurance** [James 1:2-3].

16. Suffering is a part of the mysterious process toward Christ-likeness as He also first suffered and then entered into glory (See also: Luke 24:26; Rom. 8:18; 1 Pet. 2:20-21, 5:1 and Heb. 2:10).

• [B]ut to the degree that **you share the sufferings of Christ**, keep on rejoicing, so that also at the revelation of His glory, you may rejoice with exultation [1 Pet. 4:13].

• After you have **suffered** for a little while, the God of all grace, who called you to His eternal **glory** in Christ, will Himself perfect, confirm, strengthen and establish you [1 Pet. 5:10].

The above truths give the Bible's own partial answer to why God might allow suffering or what good can come from suffering.

A full answer is never given as to why evil or pain exists. Why did God create a world that He knew would involve evil and pain? One might also ask why doesn't God finish the devil and end all sin and suffering? We wonder why God does not intervene to end man's inhumanity to fellow man (wars, crimes). Why does not God stop all accidents or natural disasters? Why does not God take a believer to heaven the moment a person trusts in Christ as Savior?

Christian philosophers suggest God allowed evil so He can destroy evil. In other words, if there had never been sin;

then sin would have remained a hypothetical possibility for eternity. By allowing sin to become a reality, God could destroy it forever.

Another common answer to the problem of evil is that God wanted to create a human race with a will to choose. God didn't want to force us to love Him. By creating humans with a choice, God knew many would chose to reject good. Yet, this tragedy is outweighed by the value of the many who do choose to trust and obey.

These two answers have some value, but they are in reality speculations. Permitting sin just to destroy it seems to make God the author of spiritual war games. Allowing evil has brought great pain. Also, human free will can help explain wars and crimes, but it does not explain weather-related tragedies, diseases, or accidents. We can blame these on Satan... (see Job 1-2; Luke 13:11,16), but then we are back to the starting point. Why did God create an anointed cherub knowing he would rebel? Why does not God stop Satan now?

Point 16 asserted that suffering makes us like Christ. The Bible repeats the pattern of suffering and glory in Christ's life.

• Was it not necessary for the Christ to **suffer** these things and to enter into His **glory**? [Luke 24:26].

• (S)eeking to know what person or time the Spirit of Christ within them was indicating as He predicted the **sufferings** of Christ and the **glories** to follow [1 Peter 1:11].

He endured suffering which led to glory, the cross then the crown. The above verses show this is the pattern God intends for a believer.

Suffering makes us more like the Lord Jesus Christ. We may also say suffering makes us more like all three Persons of the One God.

Heb. 2:9 gives the pattern of the Lord Jesus as suffering and glory:

• But we do see Him who has been made for a little while lower than the angels, namely, Jesus, because of the **suffering** of death crowned with **glory** and honor, that by the grace of God he might taste death for everyone [Heb. 2:9].

Heb. 2:10 explains that He suffered "to perfect the author of their salvation through suffering." The sinless Lord Jesus Christ could not undergo any moral improvement. Yet, suffering **improved Him** in terms of spiritual experience. There were experiences, virtues and character traits that Jesus experienced by suffering that would not have been experienced any other way. Apparently, God also allows us to suffer to bring us depth of experience and spiritual improvement.

The same passage in Hebrews compares angels and humans. Hebrews chapter one asserts Jesus is superior to angels but that He voluntarily submitted to weakness. In His human nature (He is also divine) He was lower than angels for a time. However, now He is crowned with glory and honor. The glorified human nature of Jesus has surpassed the angels. Furthermore, the Lord Jesus Christ is bringing believers through a process in which we will also surpass angels.

• Do you not know that we shall judge angels? How much more, matters of this life? [1 Cor. 6:3].

Evidently, the process of suffering in this world deepens and improves the character and spiritual experience of human beings so that believers ultimately surpass angels. By our suffering we will deserve to pass them. By living in a world of evil and pain we will have gained a depth of spiritual experience angels can never possess. By suffering we will have lived out virtues that angels never experience.

Mercy means pity for the hurting. Mercy would be forever theoretical without the existence of evil and suffering. With the existence of pain and the experience of suffering, we can experience mercy. We can also give mercy. Permitting pain to enter the universe allowed for the expression of mercy.

Longsuffering means the withholding of punishment from those who deserve it. The experience of forbearance cannot take place in moral neutrality. There is no longsuffering unless one is patient with sin. Permitting sin to enter the universe allows for the expression of longsuffering.

Grace is not just the withholding of punishment from those who deserve it. Grace is the granting of favor and kindness to those who do not deserve it. Angels have no personal experience with grace. Those who trust in Christ as Savior know God's grace. Living in a fallen world enables us to become gracious to others. Rom. 5:21 teaches, "as sin reigned in death even so grace must reign in righteousness... through Jesus Christ our Lord." If there had not been sin, could there be grace? If we had never experienced evil, could we display grace?

Love is a commitment to do what is best for another even if it hurts. True love is unconditional. Love toward those who do not love in return is supernatural, but how could this wonderful virtue ever be experienced without the existence of sin? The sin of the world caused God to display His greatest love by giving His Son to die for our sin. Those who trust in the Lord Jesus Christ experience the same sacrificial love, but could we extend sacrificial love to others unless we also at times love those who do not deserve it? How could this ever happen unless God had allowed sin so that we could love even when it hurts, even when it costs?

Forgiveness is yet another virtue that does not exist in the absence of evil. Forgiveness is a costly but a noble action. The human experience of God's forgiveness and human granting of forgiveness to others presume evil as a reality.

We can best experience and share many of God's virtues such as mercy, long-suffering, grace, and love within a world that involves evil and suffering. The theme of the entire Old Testament is that God keeps His covenants.

• Then the Lord passed by in front of him and proclaimed, "The Lord, the Lord God, compassionate and gracious, slow to anger, and **abounding in lovingkindness** and truth; **who keeps lovingkindness for thousands**, who forgives iniquity, transgression and sin; yet He will by no means leave the guilty unpunished, visiting the iniquity of fathers on the children and on the grandchildren to the third and fourth generation [Ex. 34:6-7].

The Hebrew word that refers to "keeping a covenant" is difficult to contain within one English word. The Old King James Bible translates "loving-kindness". Another phrase that communicates the idea is "loyal-love." God is loyal in His relationship to believers. He keeps His Word and promises. In many respects this world, sinful and painful, enables the practice of loyal-love to a covenant relationship. God shows His loyalty to believers by loving us despite our sin. An evil world full of pain gives us abundant opportunities to express loyalty back to God despite the test. Few things are more wonderful than complete devotion. Unless the Lord Jesus comes back in our lifetime, we are all called to give total loyalty to a God and a Savior we have never seen.

• Jesus said to him, "because you have seen Me, have you believed? Blessed are they who did not see, and yet believed"....for we walk by faith, not by sight....and though you have not seen Him, you love Him, and though you do not see Him now, but believe in Him, you greatly rejoice with joy inexpressible and full of glory [John 20:29; 2 Cor 5:7 and 1 Peter 1:8].

God has total loyal-love. He enjoys seeing it in us.

Only a fallen world enables us also to share in God's experience of giving loyal-love to other fallen creatures who sometimes cause us pain. It must give God joy to see His children keep covenants and remain in loyal-love despite the pain of a fallen and unfair world. Keeping a covenant is best experienced within marriage and family. This may explain why God ordained the home.

Angels neither marry nor are given in marriage. Why didn't God create an entire human race at once as He did angels? Because angels have no family, they can never experience God's character in keeping a covenant (loyal-love) as fully as humans can. Neither do angels experience God's love as a Creator like a good mother and father experience love for a baby they have "created." In families we practice keeping a vow and loyalty despite the test of living in a sinful world. Parents can also empathize with the example of God the Father sacrificing His Son in ways that angels can never understand. In reality, one need not be a parent to understand such pain. The loss of any beloved family member or friend causes us to understand better the idea of giving up a beloved person. Humans not angels understand the value of life and the pain of a sacrificial death. The phrase, "For God so loved the world that He gave His only begotten Son" is better understood by those who have lived in family units in a fallen and painful world.

There are few things more beautiful in life than loyalty despite all pain and costs. Without the full test of suffering, there cannot be the full measure of loyal-love. Without battle we cannot become heroic. Without experiencing evil and pain, we cannot share in the experience of God's greatest virtues.

Only a world of sin and pain followed by eternal glory allows believers to experience God fully. Angels will never share God's character traits and experience His virtues in the same way and with the same depth as humans. Therefore, in glory believers not only will surpass angels; we will deserve to surpass them. We will have become spiritually deeper and superior by our pain. Without a fallen world, many of God's great character traits would remain forever hypothetical. In a sinful and painful world, God's character has become known and shared by us. Suffering leads to glory. In eternal glory believers in the Lord Jesus Christ will forget the pain of this world but remember our present experiences of mercy, longsuffering, grace, love, forgiveness, loyalty to a covenant and a thousand other lessons that cannot be taught in a lecture but must be experienced the hard way.

DEPRESSION:

BIBLICAL CAUSES
AND
COUNSEL

Eleven sinful causes of depression
and
eight non-sinful causes of depression
taken from Scripture...
together with
Biblical sources for counsel.

This study was made for a suicide prevention effort by a Dallas police officer as he
gave talks to youth groups on weekends. It also became lecture notes for Capital
Seminary, Lanham, MD

DEPRESSION;
BIBLICAL CAUSES
AND
COUNSEL

I. Overview:

The Bible teaches us to look to our perfect God as the source of joy and meaning in life.

• **The Lord is my strength and song**, and He has become my salvation; This is my God, and I will praise Him; My father's God, and I will extol Him [Ex. 15:2].

• Then he said to them, "go, eat of the fat, drink of the sweet, and send portions to him who has nothing prepared; for this day is holy to our Lord. Do not be grieved, **for the joy of the Lord is your strength**" [Neh. 8:10].

• Let my meditation be pleasing to Him; as for me, I shall be **glad in the Lord** [Psa. 104:34].

• **The Lord is my strength and song**, and He has become my salvation [Psa. 118:14].

• The steadfast of mind Thou wilt keep **in perfect peace, because he trusts in Thee** [Isa. 26:3].

• Thus says the Lord, "Let not a wise man boast of his wisdom, and let not the mighty man boast of his might, let not a rich man boast of his riches; but **let him who boasts boast of this, that he understands and knows Me,** that I am the Lord who exercises lovingkindness, justice, and righteousness on earth; for I delight in these things," declares the Lord [Jer. 23:23-24].

• But may it never be that I should **boast**, except **in the cross** of our Lord Jesus Christ, through which the world has been crucified to me, and I to the world [Gal. 6:14].

• **Rejoice in the Lord always**; again I will say, rejoice! Let your forbearing spirit be known to all men. The Lord is near. Be anxious for nothing, but in everything by prayer and supplication with thanksgiving let your requests be made known to God. And **the peace of God**, which surpasses all comprehension, shall guard your hearts and your minds in Christ Jesus [Phil. 4:4-7].

All good in the world can be traced back to the Father, Son, and Holy Spirit who alone have perfection in attributes and works.

• **Every good thing** bestowed and every perfect gift **is from above**, coming down from the Father of lights, with whom there is no variation, or shifting shadow [James 1:17].

A focus on anything else but God is a false source of meaning and joy. It will lead to an "Ecclesiastes Syndrome" of pessimism. Nothing else can satisfy, and we eventually discover flaws and dead-ends to finding meaning in life. Human nature was created to worship God.

• Worthy art Thou, our Lord and our God, to receive glory and honor and power; for Thou didst create all things, and because of Thy will they existed, and were created [Rev. 4:11].

• And I looked, and I heard the voice of many angels around the throne and the living creatures and the elders; and the number of them was myriads and myriads, and thousands and thousands, saying with a loud voice, "worthy is the Lamb that was slain to receive power and riches and wisdom and might and honor and glory and blessing." And every created thing which is in heaven and on the earth and under the earth and on the sea, and all things in them, I heard saying, "To Him who sits on the throne, and to the Lamb, be blessing and honor and glory and dominion for ever and ever." And the four living creatures kept saying, "Amen." And the elders fell down and worshipped [Rev. 5:11-14].

Failure to give God worship and our primary attention invariably leads to feeling that life is unfulfilled and that we are being inconsistent with the core of our being.

Other things in life such as education, money, talents, achievements, sexuality within marriage, even family, cannot in themselves bring fulfillment as a substitute "god", but they can become sources of blessing when viewed as gifts from God. In a subordinate place in life, these add to our satisfaction of a flawless God (Matt. 6:33). Many of the specific causes of depression can be traced back to a failure to look to the Person and work of God as the source of meaning and joy in life.

II. Suffering Then Glory

Feeling the stress of a fallen world is part of existence. We might call this "the blues." Rom. 8:23 teaches, "we groan". 2 Corinthians 5 gives a parallel.

• For indeed while we are in this tent, we groan, being burdened, because we do not want to be unclothed, but to be clothed, in order that what is mortal may be swallowed up by life [2 Cor. 5:4].

If the alarm clock goes off and we do not feel exhilarated, we are normal. If we can't sleep, or we sleep all the time; if we can't eat or we eat all the time; if we have lost satisfaction with a perfect God; then depression is more severe and needs more attention. However, "the blues" are common to the lot of the fallen human race. We should understand that expectation of a carefree life, or constant euphoria and excitement are neither Scriptural nor true to experience. A sense of "groaning" is common.

Deeper depression might arise from the following sources:

III. Sinful Causes of Depression Contrasted with Biblical Counsel for Depression (Note: Self-attention and lack of attention to our relationship with God is common to these factors; most depressed people have multiple factors).

1. *Cause of Depression*; Guilt; example, David. Solution for this depression: for the unbeliever faith in Christ; for the believer confession of sin.

David illustrates depression arising from guilt.

• **Wash me** and I shall be whiter than snow....**Restore to me the joy of Thy salvation**, and sustain me with a willing spirit [Psa. 51:7b, 12].

• **When I kept silent about my sin**, my body wasted away through my **groaning all day long**. For day and night **Thy hand was heavy upon me**; my vitality was drained away as with the fever heat of summer, I acknowledged my sin to Thee, and my iniquity I did not hide; I said, "I will confess my transgressions to the Lord"; and Thou dost forgive the guilt of my sin....Many are the sorrows of the wicked; but he who trusts in the Lord, lovingkindness shall surround him. [Psa. 32:3-5, 10]

• O Lord, rebuke me not in Thy wrath; and chasten me not in Thy burning anger. For Thine arrows have sunk deep into me, and **Thy hand has pressed down on me.** There is no soundness in my flesh because of Thine indignation; there is no health in my bones because of my sin. For **my iniquities** are gone over my head. **As a heavy burden they weigh too much for me**. My wounds grow foul and fester. Because of my folly, I am bent over and greatly bowed down; **I go mourning all day long**. For my loins are filled with burning; and there is no soundness in my flesh. I am benumbed and badly crushed; **I groan because of the agitation of my heart**. Lord, all my desire is before Thee; and **my sighing** is not hidden from Thee. My heart throbs, my strength fails me; and the light of my eyes, even that has gone from me....**For I confess my iniquity; I am full of anxiety because of my sin** [Psa. 38:1-10,18].

King David committed adultery with Bathsheba, and she became pregnant. He then ordered his general to position Bathsheba's husband in the most dangerous part of the battle. David covered up this sin until confronted by Nathan the prophet.

Prior to confessing his sin, David grew ever more depressed. The statements quoted above refer to literal and emotional "groanings", to God's hand pressing on David, to loss of joy. David's guilt caused severe depression.

Guilt is to the soul what pain is to the body. It tells us something is wrong and must be changed. We remove guilt before God as Judge by trusting in the Lord Jesus Christ. He is God the Son who paid for our sins on the cross and rose again.

The believer who has already been forgiven by God as Judge must still confess sin to God in His role as Father. Continued unconfessed sin only leads to continued guilt and depression. Guilt and the refusal to trust in the Lord Jesus Christ (or the refusal of a believer to confess sin) is a major cause of depression.

• **How blessed is he whose transgression is forgiven**; whose sin is covered! How blessed is the man to whom the Lord does not impute iniquity....I acknowledged my sin to Thee. And my iniquity I did not hide; I said, "I will confess my transgression to the Lord"; and Thou didst forgive the guilt of my sin [Psa. 32:1-2,5].

• He who conceals his transgressions will not prosper; but he who confesses...them will find compassion [Prov. 28:13].

2.   *Cause of Depression*; Greed; example, Ahab. Solution for this depression: contentment.

Ahab illustrates depression from greed.

• So **Ahab came into his house sullen** and vexed because of the word which Naboth the Jezreelite had spoken to him; for he said, "I will not give you the inheritance of my fathers." And **he lay down on his bed and turned away his face and ate no food.** But Jezebel his wife came to him and said to him, "**how is it that your spirit is so sullen** that you are not eating food?" So he said to her, "because I spoke to Naboth the Jezreelite, and said to him, 'give me your vineyard for money; or else, if it pleases you, I will give you a vineyard in its place.' But he said, 'I will not give you my vineyard' " [1 Kings 21:4-6].

• **He who loves money will not be satisfied with money**, nor he who loves abundance with its income....The sleep of the working man is pleasant, whether he eats little or much. But the full stomach of the rich man does not allow him to sleep [Eccles. 5:10,12].

• Unless the Lord builds the house, they labor in vain who build it; unless the Lord guards the city, the watchman keeps awake in vain. It is vain for you to rise up early, to retire late, to eat the bread of painful labors; for He gives to His beloved even in his sleep [Psa. 127:1-2].

King Ahab obsessed over acquiring his neighbor's property. Because his neighbor would not sell the family lands, Ahab hid in bed and refused to eat. Advertisements barrage us with appeals to buy more and suggest we must be discontented until we acquire the product. They insist we cannot possibly be happy without it. The endless obsession with consumerism is a major cause of depression.

Society tells us contentment can only come if we have more. The Bible tells us to be content with what we have whether little or much.

• Not that I speak from want; for **I have learned to be content in whatever circumstances I am**. I know how to get along with humble means, and I also know how to live in prosperity; in any and every circumstance I have learned the secret of being filled and going hungry, both of having abundance and suffering need [Phil. 4:11-12].

• For we have brought nothing into the world, so we cannot take anything out of it either. And if we have **food and covering, with these we shall be content** [1 Tim. 6:7-8].

• Instruct those who are rich in this present world **not to be conceited or to fix their hope on the uncertainty of riches**, but on God, who richly supplies us with all things to enjoy [1 Tim. 6:17].

Viewed as ultimate satisfaction, things will only depress.

Material things viewed as gifts from God become a blessing. Many people live depressed lives because they are frustrated that they do not have more, when they could be more than content with God.

Only God is perfect. All material possessions ultimately have flaws and will disappear.

3. *Cause of Depression*; Anger; example, Cain. Solution; for *sinful* anger: confession of sin; for *righteous* anger: channel it into motivation to change the wrong and/or into a quest to ask God for His purposes.

Cain illustrates depression from anger, especially the anger of rebellion.

• But for Cain and for his offering He had no regard. So Cain **became very angry and his countenance fell**. Then the Lord said to Cain, "why are you angry?" And why has your countenance fallen? If you do well, will not your countenance be lifted up? And if you do not well, sin is crouching at the door; and its desire is for you, but you must master it [Gen. 4:5-7].

In Gen. 4:5-7 Cain became angry and "his countenance fell." Anger often leads to depression. Anger is a complex emotion. Some people direct anger at God (**the anger of rebellion**). Other times we might become angry with God because of disappointment or pain in the suffering of life (**the anger of disappointment**). Also, we frequently are angry with other people and can further divide this into **sinful anger (the anger of personal self-importance** or impatience and frustration) and **righteous anger** when God's holy laws have been violated (**the anger of God's honor**). The latter might be a situation where one or a group opposes God's work or truth, or it could involve a situation where one is personally the victim of sin.

Cain's example is actually a situation of anger at God. Heb. 11:4 says, "by faith Abel offered to God a better sacrifice..." God required **faith** (not a religion of works in a vain attempt to earn salvation). The closest modern parallel to Cain's anger would be those who rebel in anger because the real God restricts acceptance only to those who have **faith in the Lord Jesus Christ**. All other religions, philosophies, and ways of life are unacceptable. When people shake their fist at God in rebellion against His Son, they will experience depression. **The solution is faith in Christ as Savior.**

A believer might rebel against God's commands with disrespect and anger. This will also cause ones "countenance to fall." The anger of rebellion brings depression to believers until such sins are confessed as sin.

Sometimes we become angry with God because of suffering in life. We might call this the anger of disappointment rather than the anger of rebellion. The Bible gives examples of respectful "venting":

• Have I sinned? What have I done to Thee, O watcher of men? Why hast Thou set me as Thy target, so that I am a burden to myself....According to Thy knowledge I am indeed not guilty; yet there is no deliverance from Thy hand....Know then that God has wronged me, and has closed His net around me [Job 7:20, 10:7, 19:6].

• How long, O Lord? Wilt Thou forget me forever? How long wilt Thou hide Thy face from me? [Psa. 13:1].

• O Lord, Thou hast deceived me and I was deceived; Thou hast overcome me and prevailed. I have become a laughingstock all day long; everyone mocks me [Jer. 20:7].

If one quickly channels these emotions into a search for understanding, then God tolerates our being upset. Even the Lord Jesus asked, "Why?"

• My God, my God, why hast Thou forsaken me?" Far from my deliverance are the words of my groaning....And about the ninth hour Jesus cried out with a loud voice, saying, "Eli, Eli, lama sabachthani?" that is, "My God, my God, why hast Thou forsaken me?" [Psa. 22:1; Matt. 27:46].

However, Isa. 40:27 shows that being upset with God must be channeled into a quest for deeper understanding of His ways and not be allowed to become anger in the sense of disrespectful rebellion.

• Why do you say, O Jacob, and assert, O Israel, my way is hidden from the Lord, and the justice due me escapes the notice of my God? [Isa. 40:27].

Anger directed at God causes depression. So does anger directed at other people. Sometimes people transfer their anger with God to other people. Cain did this to Abel. Sometimes the person transfers anger directed at God to his/her family or pastor.

Sinful anger responds to an offense against personal self-importance and is hasty.

• The Lord is compassionate and gracious, **slow to anger** and abounding in lovingkindness [Psa. 103:8].

• He who is **slow to anger** has great understanding, but he who is quick-tempered exalts folly [Prov. 14:29].

•...but let everyone be quick to hear, slow to speak and **slow to anger** [James 1:19].

Sinful anger is the anger of personal insult or impatience. The offense does not involve an attack upon God or a serious violation of His laws. We often rationalize and categorize all anger as being righteous indignation. However, much anger does not really involve a violation of God's holy standards. We become angry over waiting in line or flat tires. We get mad at the human limitations of others or from misunderstanding them. Much anger is sinful and should be confessed as sin. If not, we risk depression.

Some anger is righteous indignation. God's person and work have been insulted or opposed, or an individual has been the victim of a serious sin. God was angry with those who worshiped the golden calf.

• Now then let Me alone, that My anger may burn against them, and that I may destroy them [Ex. 32:10a].

Jesus was angry with those lacking compassion for a man with a crippled hand.

• And after looking around at them with anger, grieved at their hardness of heart, He said to the man, "Stretch out your hand..."[Mark 3:5a].

Righteous anger against enemies of the faith **should be channeled into motivation** to protect others from their errors. Rebuke might be in order, but it is the type of rebuke that is motivated to help others by reducing sin's destruction. In other words, we oppose people because we love them and do not want to see them harmed because of their false views or sins. Eph. 4:26-27 and James 1:19-20 teach that we must handle righteous indignation carefully or it leads to sin, e.g. hatred, bitterness.

• Be angry, and yet do not sin; do not let the sun go down on your anger, and do not give the devil an opportunity [Eph. 4:26-27].

• This you know, my beloved brethren. But let everyone be quick to hear, slow to speak and slow to anger; for the anger of man does not achieve the righteousness of God [James 1:19-20].

"The anger of man does not achieve the righteousness of God." Righteous anger must be channeled into motivation to oppose evil in ways that show love for evildoers. The Lord's example seems to have given more patience and grace with sinners and stronger rebuke to those leading others into sin.

Righteous anger might involve generic opposition to groups that oppose God or their leaders. It can also be a personal response when one becomes a victim of another's sin (see pages 45-49, which deal with handling the offense of being the target of a wrong). In most cases, we will be better off emotionally by forgiving an offense even if there is no request for forgiveness. "Love covers a multitude of sins".

• Above all, keep fervent in your love for one another, because love covers a multitude of sins [1 Pet. 4:8].

• A man's discretion makes him slow to anger, and it is his glory to overlook transgression [Prov. 19:11].

Also, the Bible never allows hatred. While resistance to an evil act in progress is morally acceptable; revenge for past wrongs is not.

• Deliver those who are being taken away to death, and those who are staggering to slaughter, Oh hold them back. If you say, "see, we did not know this," does He not consider it who weighs the hearts? And does He not know it who keeps your soul? And will He not render to man according to His work? [Prov. 24:11-12].

Hatred and seeking revenge are certain ways to depression. With serious sins, God allows one who has been grieved to seek repentance and hold another morally accountable.

We do not have the option to hate, but we can seek restoration through repentance and perhaps church discipline (God gives the state the authority for justice in criminal sins).

• And if your brother sins, go and reprove him in private; if he listens to you, you have won your brother. But if he does not listen to you, take one or two more with you, so that by the mouth of two or three witnesses every fact may be confirmed. And if he refuses to listen to them, tell it to the church; and if he refuses to listen even to the church, let him be to you as a gentile and a tax-gatherer [Matt. 18:15-17].

If a sin is too serious to overlook and cover, then we can hold another morally accountable by rebuke and seeking repentance. We can go to the church to ask for discipline and to

the government for justice. However, if these fail, we must turn
the matter over to God as Jesus did when He was wronged.

• ...Christ also suffered for you, leaving an example for you to
follow....and while being reviled, He did not revile in return;
while suffering He uttered no threats, but kept entrusting
Himself to Him who judges righteously [1 Pet. 2:21b, 23].

        Sinful anger leads to depression. We must confess and
forsake it. *Righteous* anger should be changed into motivation
to right the wrong and/or a search to understand God's
purposes.

        4.   *Cause of Depression*; Hatred; examples, Jonah and
Haman. Solution for this depression: love.

        Jonah hated the people of Nineveh and ended up in suicidal
depression. Wicked Haman hated the Jews and was unhappy
despite many advantages in life.

• **But it greatly displeased Jonah, and he became angry**.
And he prayed to the Lord and said, "please Lord, was this not
what I said while I was still in my own country? Therefore, in
order to forestall this I fled to Tarshish, for I knew that Thou
art a gracious and compassionate God, slow to anger and
abundant in lovingkindness, and one who relents concerning
calamity. Therefore now, O Lord, **please take my life from
me, for death is better to me than life." And the Lord said,
"do you have good reason to be angry?"**....And it came
about when the sun came up that God appointed a scorching
east wind, and the sun beat down on Jonah's head so that he
became faint and **begged with all his soul to die, saying,
"Death is better to me than life."** [Jonah 4:1-4, 8-9].

• Then Haman recounted to them the glory of his riches, and the number of his sons, and every instance where the king had magnified him, and how he had promoted him above the princes and servants of the king. Haman also said, "Even Esther the queen let no one but me come with the king to the banquet which she had prepared; and tomorrow also I am invited by her with the king. **Yet all of this does not satisfy me every time I see Mordecai the Jew** sitting at the king's gate" [Esther 5:11-13].

Jonah was suicidal because God saved the hated Assyrians. Haman told his wife he had riches, high position, and a large family, but none of this brought joy the moment he saw Mordecai the Jew.

If we hate someone and watch him or her succeed in life, we will be depressed. Though we might need to oppose and rebuke and even withhold forgiveness (in the sense of holding another morally accountable), hatred causes us depression. We benefit in obeying Matt. 5:44.

• But I say to you, love your enemies, and pray for those who persecute you [Matt. 5:44].

The obsession for vengeance brings depression and is not a Christian option.

• Never take your own revenge, beloved, but leave room for the wrath of God, for it is written, "Vengeance is mine, I will repay," says the Lord. But if your enemy is hungry, feed him, and if he is thirsty, give him a drink; for in so doing you will heap burning coals upon his head [Rom. 12:19-20].

• Do not say, "I will repay evil"; wait for the Lord, and He will save you…. [Prov. 20:22].

• Do not say, "Thus I shall do to him as he has done to me; I will render to the man according to his work." [Prov. 24:29].

Love is obviously the opposite of hatred. Those who admire the Lord Jesus Christ will want to become like Him, and this involves overcoming hatred.

• We love, because He first loved us. If someone says, "I love God," and hates his brother, he is a liar, for the one who does not love his brother whom he has seen, cannot love God whom he has not seen. And this commandment we have from Him, that the one who loves God should love his brother also [1 John 4:19-21].

5. *Cause of Depression*; Perfectionism, self-imposed unrealistic expectations; example, Moses. Solution for this depression: self-acceptance of human limitations.

Moses could not control the children of Israel or create an ideal nation. Even Moses thought of suicide because of his perfectionism.

• So Moses said to the Lord, **"why hast Thou been so hard on Thy servant**? And why have I not found favor in Thy sight, that Thou hast laid the burden of all this people on me? Was it I who conceived all this people? Was it I who brought them forth, that Thou shouldst say to me, 'carry them in your bosom as a nurse carries a nursing infant, to the land which Thou didst swear to their fathers'? Where am I to get meat to give to all this people? For they weep before me saying, 'give us meat that we may eat!' **I alone am not able to carry all this people**, because it is too burdensome to me. So if Thou art going to deal thus with me, **please kill me at once**, if I have found favor in Thy sight, and do not let me see my wretchedness" [Num. 11:11-15].

- Unless the Lord builds the house, they labor in vain who build it; unless the Lord guards the city, the watchman keeps awake in vain. **It is vain for you to rise up early, to retire late, to eat the bread of painful labors**; for He gives to His beloved even in His sleep [Psa. 127:1-2].

     Excellence is a virtue but perfectionism is cruel and produces depression. Moses was suicidal because he could neither control nor please the children of Israel. The solution is to accept our human limitations and accept God's grace for our flaws.

- Lord, make me to know my end, and what is the extent of my days, let me know how transient I am....For He Himself knows our frame; He is mindful that we are but dust [Psa. 39:4, 103:14].

     Unless an issue is a Biblical point of morality, we might need to refuse the judgment others make against us, as Paul did in 1 Corinthians. Paul told Timothy and Titus there were limits to the criticism they had to take.

- But to me it is a very small thing that I should be examined by you, or by any human court; in fact, I do not even examine myself [1 Cor. 4:3].

- Let no one despise your youth...[1 Tim. 4:12 KJV].

- Let no one disregard you [Titus 2:15].

     We strive for excellence but must admit weakness.

- Not that I have already obtained it, or have already become perfect, but I press on in order that I may lay hold of that for which also I was laid hold of by Christ Jesus [Phil. 3:12].

"There is a God. I am not He." Striving for excellence
is a virtue. Perfectionistic demands on self are depressing. One
might classify the perfectionistic mindset as non-sinful as we
are mostly taught it by others. However, if we realize the
danger of unrealistic self-expectations but refuse to adjust, then
trying to be perfect to the point of depression would be a sin.

6.   *Cause of Depression*; Fear: examples, Elijah, Saul.
Solution for such depression: trust in God, acceptance of God's
unconditional love.

Elijah and Saul both illustrate that fear causes depression.

• Then Jezebel sent a messenger to **Elijah**, saying, "so may the
gods do to me and even more, if I do not make your life as the
one of them by tomorrow about this time." And **he was afraid
and arose and ran for his life** and came to Beersheba, which
belongs to Judah, and left his servant there. But he himself
went a day's journey into the wilderness, and came and sat
down under a juniper tree; and **he requested for himself that
he might die, and said, "it is enough; now, O Lord, take my
life**, for I am not better than my fathers" [1 Kings 19:2-4].

• Now **Saul was afraid of David,** for the Lord was with him,
but had departed from Saul....then **Saul was even more afraid**
of David. Thus Saul was David's enemy continually [1 Sam.
18:12, 29].

The Bible teaches that worry over money also causes
depression.

• It is vain for you to rise up early, to retire late, to eat the
bread of painful labors; for He gives to His beloved…[Psa.
127:2].

• The sleep of the working man is pleasant, whether he eats little or much. But the full stomach of the rich man does not allow him to sleep [Eccles. 5:12].

Unbelievers face depression because of life's uncertainty and a hopeless eternal destiny. Christians have an advantage because a believer's way of life includes belief in a God who cares for every need and superintends every event. However, often even Christians do not live as if God controls their lives. The Psalmist said increased hope in God is a solution for a downcast soul.

• Why are you **in despair, O my soul**? And why have you become disturbed within me? **Hope in God**, for I shall again praise Him for the **help of His presence** [Psa. 42:5].

• Therefore be not anxious for tomorrow; for tomorrow will take care of itself. Each day has enough trouble of its own [Matt. 6:34].

• **Be anxious for nothing**, but in everything by prayer and supplication with thanksgiving let your requests be made known to God. **And the peace of God**, which surpasses all comprehension, **shall guard your hearts and your minds** in Christ Jesus [Phil. 4:6-7].

• (C)asting all your anxiety on Him, because He cares for you [1 Pet. 5:7].

• There is no fear in love; but perfect love casts out fear, because fear involves punishment, and the one who fears is not perfected in love [1 John 4:18].

The solution for depression based on fear is faith in a God who watches over our needs and provides.

7. *Cause of Depression*; Jealousy; example, Saul.
Solution for such depression: unselfishness, focusing on God's
honor and viewing any honor for self as God's concern.

Saul illustrates that depression can arise from jealousy.

• And it happened as they were coming, when David returned
from killing the Philistine, that the women came out of all the
cities of Israel, singing and dancing, to meet King Saul with
tambourines, with joy and with musical instruments. And the
women sang as they played, and said, **"Saul has slain his
thousands, and David his ten thousands.**" Then Saul became
very angry, for this saying displeased him; and he said, **"they
have ascribed to David ten thousands, but to me they have
ascribed thousands.** Now what more can he have but the
kingdom?" And Saul looked at David with suspicion from that
day on. Now it came about on the next day that an evil spirit
from God came mightily upon Saul, and he raved in the midst
of his house, while David was playing the harp with his hand,
as usual; and a spear was in Saul's hand. And Saul hurled the
spear for he thought, "I will pin David to the wall." But David
escaped from his presence twice. Now Saul was afraid of
David, for the Lord was with him, for the Lord was with him
but had departed from Saul....**when Saul saw that he was
prospering greatly, he dreaded him**. [1 Sam. 18:6–12, 15].

     Saul became depressed from the moment he heard the
chant, "Saul has killed thousands, but David has killed tens of
thousands." Jealousy is fundamentally selfishness or pride. The
connection between jealousy and depression is obvious.
Whether the object of our jealousy succeeds by evil schemes or
by God's blessing, we become depressed as we watch others
advance. We should not envy the "success" of the wicked.
Neither should we envy the advance of the righteous. Their
blessing is a cause for joy not jealousy.

• Do not fret because of evildoers, be not envious toward wrongdoers. For they will wither quickly like the grass, and fade like the green herb. Trust in the Lord, and do good; dwell in the land and cultivate faithfulness. Delight yourself in the Lord; and He will give you the desires of your heart. Commit your way to the Lord, trust also in Him, and He will do it [Psa. 37:1-5].

• But as for me, my feet came close to stumbling; my steps had almost slipped. For I was envious of the arrogant, as I saw the prosperity of the wicked....If I had said, "I will speak thus," behold, I should have betrayed the generation of Thy children. When I pondered to understand this, it was troublesome in my sight until I came into the sanctuary of God; then I perceived their end [Psa.73:2-3, 15-18].

Again, the solution is contentment in a perfect God and entrusting our lives to Him. There is a difference between **purpose and result. The purpose of life should be to honor and promote God not to honor self.**

• But may it never be that I should boast, except in the cross of our Lord Jesus Christ, through which the world has been crucified to me, and I to the world [Gal. 6:14].

Living for God may even **result** in honor in this life but that outcome is God's business not our purpose for trying. God controls exaltation. We need not become jealous of those who advance nor should we become vain if *we* have success. Though our hard work and skills may be an element to success, God's blessing is necessary to ultimate success.

If we have setbacks and disappointments, God has allowed them for a good purpose.

• For not from the east, nor from the west, nor from the desert comes exaltation; but God is the Judge; He puts down one, and exalts another [Psa. 75:6-7].

• For who regards you as superior? And what do you have that you did not receive? But if you did receive it, why do you boast as if you had not received it? [1 Cor. 4:7].

We should live to promote and honor God.

• And you shall love the Lord your God with all your heart and with all your soul and with all your might [Deut. 6:5].

• Thus says the Lord, "Let not a wise man boast of his wisdom, and let not the mighty man boast of his might, let not a rich man boast of his riches; but let him who boasts boast of this, that he understands and knows Me, that I am the Lord who exercises lovingkindness, justice, and righteousness on earth; for I delight in these things," declares the Lord [Jer. 9:23-24].

God provides honor for the godly (1 Sam. 2:30) but how and when He honors us is His decision. It is not our focus or concern as we concentrate on honoring Him. In some cases, God will choose to reserve most or even all honor for the next life with increased reward in heaven (though we are saved by grace through faith alone).

• A man's pride will bring him low, but a humble spirit will obtain honor [Prov. 29:23].

• For everyone who exalts himself will be humbled, and he who humbles himself will be exalted....I tell you, this man went down to his house justified rather than the other; for everyone who exalts himself will be humbled, but he who humbles himself will be exalted [Luke 14:11, 18:14].

• Humble yourselves in the presence of the Lord, and He will exalt you [James 4:10].

• Humble yourselves, therefore, under the mighty hand of God, that He may exalt you at the proper time [1 Peter 5:6].

Since jealousy is a form of pride and since God exalts the humble, jealousy is a sure way to fail to obtain God's approval and promotion. We just get depressed. Again, love is a contradiction of jealousy. Loving the brethren would mean we rejoice at accomplishments in a spiritual person's life.

• Rejoice with those who rejoice, and weep with those who weep [Rom. 12:15].

8. *Cause for Depression*; Laziness. Solution for such depression: productivity.

• (M)oreover, that every man who eats and drinks sees good in all his **labor – it is the gift of God**....and I have seen that **nothing is better than that man should be happy with his activities**, for that is his lot. For who will bring him to see what will occur after him?....Here is what I have seen to be good and fitting: to eat, drink and **enjoy oneself in all one's labor** in which he toils under the sun during the few years of his life which God has given him; for this is his reward. Furthermore, as for every man to whom God has given riches and wealth, He has empowered him to eat from them and to receive his reward and **rejoice in his labor**; this is the gift of God [Eccles. 3:13,22; 5:18-19].

While overwork can be perfectionistic and lead to depression, laziness also causes depression. We feel unproductive and wasted. Even the semi-humanistic perspective of Ecclesiastes leads to the conclusion that work is a gift of God.

9.   Cause for Depression; rejection of the Anointed One; example, Judas. Solution for such depression: faith in Christ.

Ahithophel betrayed King David and later became so depressed he killed himself. He is a type of Judas who also betrayed his Master and King with the same depressing outcome.

• Now when Ahithophel saw that his counsel was not followed, he saddled his donkey and arose and went to his home, to his city, and **set his house in order, and strangled himself**; thus he died and was buried in the grave of his father [2 Sam. 17:23].

• And he threw the pieces of silver into the sanctuary and departed; and **he went away and hanged himself** [Matt. 27:5].

Both Ahithophel, the type (Psa. 41:9) and Judas the fulfillment (John 13:18) died in depression. It is not possible to reject Christ as Savior and escape depression. There would be a parallel application for believers who by definition have not totally rejected Christ but may reject His commands and will for their lives.

10. *Cause for depression*; Distorted sexuality, example, Amnon. Solution for such depression: sex viewed as God's gift within marriage.

David's son, Amnon, felt that a twisted sexual relationship with his half-sister, Tamar, would give him satisfaction in life. He raped her and was just as unhappy as ever.

• Now it was after this that Absalom the son of David had a beautiful sister whose name was Tamar, and Amnon the son of David loved her. And Amnon was so frustrated because of his sister Tamar that he made himself ill, for she was a virgin, and it seemed hard to Amnon to do anything to her. But Amnon had a friend whose name was Jonadab, the son of Shimeah, David's brother; and Jonadab was a very shrewd man. And he said to him, "O son of the king, **why are you so depressed morning after morning**? Will you not tell me?" Then Amnon said to him, "**I am in love** with Tamar, the sister of my brother Absalom"....However, he would not listen to her; since he was stronger than she, he violated her and lay with her. Then Amnon hated her with a very great hatred; for the hatred with which he hated her was greater than the love with which he had loved her. And Amnon said to her, "get up, go away!" [2 Sam. 13:1-4, 14, 15].

God created us as sexual beings, and the Bible actually commands married couples to enjoy each other. However, the same fire that warms can also burn. Not only do many people disregard God's commands intended for our emotional safety, some also act as if sex becomes a "god." In many cases people think if they can find a different partner, a different practice, or a new perversion, they will finally obtain satisfaction in life. Outside of a faithful commitment in marriage, sexual experimentation, whether of a normal heterosexual variety or twisted practices, will end in frustration and depression. Sex as God's gift within His control is a gift and blessing. However, sex makes a terrible god or reason for existence.

The best Bible story that illustrates this is probably unfamiliar because it is so scandalous. David's firstborn son, Amnon, could have been the next king of Israel. Instead the spoiled, rotten prince developed a twisted sexual fascination for his half-sister, Tamar. 2 Samuel 13:2 says, Amnon made himself sick lusting for Tamar. One of his friends asked, "O son of the king, why are you so depressed morning after morning?" Amnon replied that he loved his sister. He devised a plan to rape Tamar after pretending sickness and asking her to bring a meal to his bedroom. After the rape Amnon realized his conquest brought no satisfaction. His twisted sexual experience brought no joy.

Those who rebel against God's guidance in matters of sexuality and falsely think sex alone gives meaning to life will share Amnon's frustration. When our sexuality is given a subordinate place in life and viewed as a gift given and controlled by God, then it too can contribute to satisfaction in life. As a god, it is depressing.

11.   *Cause for Depression*; Occult influence; solution for such depression: reject all involvement with New Age practices.

The demonic overlaps with suicide and depression.

• Now the Spirit of the Lord departed from Saul, and an evil spirit from the Lord terrorized him [1 Sam. 16:14].

• And constantly night and day, among the tombs and in the mountains, he was crying out and gashing himself with stones....And they brought the boy to Him. And when He saw him, immediately the spirit threw him into a convulsion, and falling to the ground, he began rolling about and foaming at the mouth....and it has often thrown him both into the fire and into the water to destroy him [Mark 5:5, 9:20, 22a].

God is the source of joy. Satan and his angels bring the antithesis of joy. We **must reject the occult**.

IV.   Non-sinful Causes of Depression Contrasted with Biblical Counsel

1. *Cause for depression*; Being a victim of sin; examples, Jesus and the Hebrews as slaves. Counsel for such depression; forgiveness.

The Lord Jesus Christ seemed depressed in the Garden of Gethsemane the night before His death on the cross. The children of Israel were depressed because of Pharaoh's cruel mistreatment.

• Then He said to them, "My soul is deeply grieved, to the point of death; remain here and keep watch with Me" [Matt. 26:38].

• So Moses spoke thus to the sons of Israel, but they did not listen to Moses on account of their despondency and cruel bondage [Ex. 6:9].

A child abandoned by father or mother, a person falsely accused, a crime victim, and other victims of sin will tend to feel depression. This type of depression is a non-sinful and normal response. Yet, it might lead to sin if an innocent victim responds with bitterness, disregards life's responsibilities, or loses satisfaction in God.

The solution to depression for a moral offense is forgiveness, but forgiveness must be carefully defined to prevent misunderstanding. Some Bible texts emphasize the emotional aspects of forgiveness.

• And whenever you stand praying, forgive, if you have anything against anyone; so that your Father also who is in heaven may forgive your transgressions....Never pay back evil for evil to anyone. Respect what is right in the sight of all men. If possible, so far as it depends upon you, be at peace with all men. Never take your own revenge, beloved, but leave room for the wrath of God, for it is written, "vengeance is mine, I will repay", says the Lord. But if your enemy is hungry, feed him, and if he is thirsty, give him a drink; for in so doing, you will heap burning coals upon his head" [Mark 11:25; Rom. 12:17-20].

The opposite of forgiveness would be hatred and revenge. If defined in an emotional sense, it is always right and psychologically beneficial for the victim to forgive. However, the original Hebrew and Greek words for forgiveness stress the definition of moral/legal accountability. If stress is upon accountability, forgiveness means to remove a crushing burden, to cancel a debt, or to drop the charge against another. While it is always right and best to forgive in the sense of rejecting vengeance and hatred, the Bible does allow the option of withholding forgiveness in the sense of holding another morally accountable. The government should, for example, hold serious evildoers accountable.

• (F)or it (authority) is a minister of God to you for good. But if you do what is evil, be afraid; for it does not bear the sword for nothing; for it is a minister of God, an avenger who brings wrath upon the one who practices evil [Rom. 13:4].

In addition, on a personal level a Christian also has the right to go in private and seek repentance.

• And if your brother sins, go and reprove him in private; if he listens to you, you have won your brother. But if he does not listen to you, take one or two more with you, so that by the mouth of two or three witnesses every fact may be confirmed. And if he refuses to listen to them, tell it to the church; and if he refuses to listen even to the church, let him be to you as a gentile and a tax gatherer [Matt. 18:15-17].

The Bible allows us to seek an explanation or apology for wrong but also cautions we should do so quickly to prevent seething in bitterness.

• Be angry, and yet do not sin; do not let the sun go down on your anger, and do not give the devil an opportunity [Eph. 4:26-27].

If the offender will not confess or reconcile after several attempts, it might be necessary to withdraw from this relationship to prevent further pain, including depression.

Christian love and graciousness demand that we frequently forgive others without even being asked. We should always reject vengeance and should overlook most offenses.

• A man's discretion makes him slow to anger, and it is his glory to overlook a transgression [Prov. 19:11].

• Above all, keep fervent in your love for one another, because love conquers a multitude of sins [1 Pet. 4:8.].

• (B)earing with one another, and forgiving each other, whoever has a complaint against anyone; just as the Lord forgave you, so also should you [Col. 3:13].

• (W)ith all humility and gentleness, with patience, showing forbearance to one another in love [Eph. 4:2].

Though we may never hate, nevertheless with serious evil acts we might hold another morally accountable and seek to obtain confession and repentance. The outcome will either be confession and repentance leading to complete forgiveness or a continued breach in the relationship. In the latter case, we must eventually leave the matter to God.

In the long term a Christian is wise to resolve all issues within his or her soul by giving full forgiveness even if attempts to hold another accountable fail and the relationship is permanently damaged. We have the right to seek an apology, and to support the state in prosecuting crimes, but we will be better off emotionally by eventually granting forgiveness in both the emotional and moral accountability sense after attempts to seek repentance and perhaps also justice through the state. Continued efforts to seek an apology from an unreasonable person would only increase the likelihood of depression. We must never hate, and sometimes God alone will have to enforce moral accountability. God has the wisdom and power to address the wrong fairly in His time and way. At some point, therefore, everyone who has been wronged should forgive, even if only for the emotional benefit forgiveness brings. We might even need to forgive the dead or those with whom we have lost contact.

Our sin victimized the Lord Jesus and caused His soul to become "sorrowful unto death"; and He handled His victimization with forgiveness.

• Then He said to them, "My soul is deeply grieved, to the point of death; remain here and keep watch with Me"....but Jesus was saying, "Father, forgive them; for they do not know what they are doing" [Matt. 26:38; Luke 23:34)].

Entrusting oneself to God sustains us when wronged.

•...Christ also suffered for you, leaving an example for you to follow....and while being reviled, He did not revile in return; while suffering He uttered no threats, but kept entrusting Himself to Him who judges righteously [1 Pet. 2:21, 23].

We must never hate, and sometimes God alone will have to enforce moral accountability. God has the wisdom and power to address the wrong fairly in His time and way.

2. *Cause for Depression*; False guilt. Counsel for such depression: true Biblical standards of good and evil, acceptance of God's forgiveness.

False guilt refers to feelings of guilt that occur when one has not committed a Biblical sin. One who kills another in an accident or one who decides to put a relative in a nursing home will feel guilt even when no actual evil has been committed. 1 John 3:20 helps with false guilt, "For if our heart condemn us, God is greater than our heart and knoweth all things" (KJV). We might feel guilty for a mishap or even being sinned against (such as the children of divorce who often experience false guilt), but God knows such things are not wrong.

Legalism also produces false guilt in many Christian circles. We feel guilty for things the Bible does not even address because others judge us by purely man-made standards. Both types of false guilt may be alleviated by careful study of what the Bible actually defines as sin.

A third type of false guilt occurs when one confesses sin but continues to feel guilt by not accepting God's forgiveness. Paul advises us to move on from past sins that have been forgiven.

• Brethren, I do not regard myself as having laid hold of it yet; but one thing I do: **forgetting** what lies behind and reaching forward to what lies ahead…[Phil. 3:13].

3. *Cause for Depression*; Rejection, unfair criticism, betrayal. Counsel for such depression: security in God's love and grace, obey God then develop a "thick-skin".

The Lord Jesus Christ understands rejection more than anyone. Rejection caused Him much sorrow, including emotional sorrow (Isaiah 53). Perhaps King David shows the relationship between rejection and depression. When leaving Jerusalem after Absalom's rebellion, he did not care when enemies cursed and threw stones (2 Samuel 16). Moses' depression was partly from his own perfectionist tendencies but also from unfair criticism and rejection of his leadership (see the context leading to Num. 11:11-15, especially 11:1,4-6,10,12).

• Now the people became like those who complain of adversity in the hearing of the Lord; and when the Lord heard it, His anger was kindled, and the fire of the Lord burned among them and consumed some of the outskirts of the camp....and the rabble who were among them had greedy desires; and also the sons of Israel wept again and said, "who will give us meat to eat? We remember the fish which we used to eat free in Egypt, the cucumbers and the melons and the leeks and the onions and the garlic, but now our appetite is gone. There is nothing to look at except this manna"....now Moses heard the people weeping throughout their families, each man at the doorway of his tent; and the anger of the Lord was kindled greatly, and Moses was displeased....Was it I who conceived all this people? Was it I who brought them forth, that Thou shouldst say to me, "carry them in your bosom as a nurse carries a nursing infant, to the land which Thou didst swear to their fathers?....please kill me at once" [Num. 11:1, 4-6, 10,12,15].

Renewed focus on a perfect God (and a perfect book, God's Word) helps overcome depression from rejection or criticism. Jeremiah had much rejection and depression.

• Cursed be the day when I was born; let the day not be blessed when my mother bore me! Cursed be the man who brought the news to my father, saying, "a baby boy has been born to you!" [Jer. 20:14-15].

Jeremiah endured rejection by attention upon the perfections of God.

• Thus says the Lord, "let not a wise man boast of his wisdom, and let not the mighty man boast of his might, let not a rich man boast of his riches; but let him who boasts **boast of this, that he understands and knows Me**, that I am the Lord who exercises lovingkindness, justice, and righteousness on earth…" [Jer. 9:23-24].

Jeremiah also endured being treated unfairly by taking joy in God's perfect Book, the Bible.

• Woe to me, my mother, that you have borne me as a man of strife and a man of contention to all the land! I have neither lent, nor have men lent money to me, yet everyone curses me….You who know, O Lord, remember me, take notice of me, and take vengeance for me on my persecutors. Do not, in view of Your patience, take me away; know that for Your sake I endure reproach. Your words were found and I ate them, and **Your words became for me a joy and the delight of my heart; for I have been called by Your name**, O Lord God of hosts. I did not sit in the circle of merrymakers, nor did I exult. Because of your hand upon me I sat alone, for You filled me with indignation [Jer. 15:10, 15-17].

Jeremiah could endure unfair treatment and rejection by focusing on a perfect God and a perfect Book. He also took comfort in the call of God to serve in the Lord's work. In a sense, all believers have a similar calling from God that can sustain even when life is unfair.

• O Lord, Thou hast deceived me and I was deceived; Thou hast overcome me and prevailed. I have become a laughingstock all day long; everyone mocks me. For each time I speak, I cry aloud; I proclaim violence and destruction, because for me the word of the Lord has resulted in reproach and derision all day long. **But if I say, "I will not remember Him or speak anymore in His Name", then in my heart it becomes like a burning fire shut up in my bones**; and I am weary of holding it in, and I cannot endure it [Jer. 20:7-9].

God's approval of our work matters more than unfair criticism from fussy people.

• **Let them curse, but do Thou bless**; when they arise, they shall be ashamed, but Thy servant shall be glad....with my mouth I will give thanks abundantly to the Lord; and in the midst of many I will praise Him. **For He stands at the right hand of the needy, to save him from those who judge his soul** [Psa. 109:28, 30-31].

In helping others who have been hurt by rejection, God's servants should stress the doctrine of grace (God's acceptance of our weakness), the example of Christ (see Isaiah 53, 1 Pet. 2:21-23), and the practice of encouragement. When unfairly criticized, we might need to follow Paul's example and refuse (at least in our own minds) others the right to judge in areas where the Bible is silent and on matters that are not so much sin as human limitations.

• **But to me it is a very small thing that I should be examined by you**, or by any human court; in fact, I do not even examine myself [1 Cor. 4:3].

Turn the critical words over to God.

• Cast your burden upon the Lord, and He will sustain you; He will never allow the righteous to be shaken....casting all your anxiety upon Him, because He cares for you [Psa. 55:22; 1 Peter 5:7].

4. *Cause for Depression*; Dashed hopes, failure of plans, or false expectations. Counsel for depression: a motivation to glorify God and leaving results to God.

Some impossible dreams may remain unfulfilled but pleasing God **is** attainable. One of the factors in Elijah's depression was the failure of an anticipated revival after defeating the Baal prophets at Mt. Carmel in 1 Kings 18. 1 Kings 19:4,10 "It is enough, now, O Lord, take my life, for I am no better than my fathers....I have been very zealous for the Lord...the sons of Israel have forsaken Thy covenant..." Elijah was depressed because the nation would not turn to God despite the prophet's hard work and prayers.

The goal of faithfulness to the Lord Jesus Christ is attainable. Sometimes other of life's dreams and goals are not (even David never built the Temple). Some dreams might fail. Realization of the true goal in life helps. We should strive to hear the Lord's "well done..." (Matt. 25:21,23) and to be faithful whatever the results.

• In this case, moreover, it is required of stewards that one be found trustworthy [1 Cor. 4:2].

We can offer the best sacrifice of labor but results are out of our control. Isaiah was excited about ministry after discovering God's holiness. He was eager to be sent. Yet, God told him the nation was blind (Isaiah 6). Isaiah could work until he dropped, but there would be limited results. His real reward was God Himself. The prodigal son's older brother focused so much on life's work that he forgot to enjoy the father and worked with a bad attitude. Faithfulness is obtainable. Other goals in life might or might not come to pass. In eternity the faithfulness will matter far more than the level of visible successes of the present.

5. *Cause for Depression*; Trying to meet other's ungracious or unrealistic expectations. Counsel for such depression: living by God's standards, not trying to please everyone.

While this cause of depression is a form of perfectionism, trying to please fussy people concerns the effort to attain unfair or legalistic expectations others impose upon us. Perfectionism might more directly involve self-imposed expectations. Col. 3:21 tells fathers "...do not exasperate your children so that they will not lose heart." Unrealistic or ungracious standards in the home, church, business, or society can cause depression among those well-intentioned who loyally try to meet someone's impossible demands. God's Word is the measure of virtue and excellence. Others can be harsh critics. The desire to please unreasonable people causes depression, but God's commands are often easier than people's expectations. His real commands are neither unreasonable nor a burden.

• Come to Me, all who are weary and heavy-laden, and I will give you rest. Take My yoke upon you, and learn from Me, for I am gentle and humble in heart; and you shall find rest for your souls...**For My yoke is easy, and my burden is light** [Matt. 11:28, 30].

• For this is the love of God, that we keep His commandments; and **His commandments are not burdensome** [1 John 5:3].

God's commands protect us from sin's harm. They are for our benefit. Following actual **Biblical standards** for evaluation and **refusal to worry about judgmental people** helps with depression.

• But to me it is a very small thing that I should be examined by you, or by any human court; in fact, I do not even examine myself [Paul, 1 Cor. 4:3].

Grace involves tolerating other people's flaws and even some sins. Often crabby people are really upset with God or insecure or have problems unrelated to the person they attack in their misdirected venting.

• (B)earing with one another, and forgiving each other, whoever has a complaint against anyone; just as the Lord forgave you, so also should you....with all humility and gentleness, with patience, showing forbearance to one another in love [Col. 3:13; Eph. 4:2).

We might need to rebuke others for their unrealistic expectations or unfairness toward us. The Bible allows for this but tells us to exercise this option with love and humility.

• Brethren, even if a man is caught in any trespass, you who are spiritual, restore such a one in a spirit of gentleness; each one looking to yourself, lest you too be tempted. Bear one another's burdens, and thus fulfill the law of Christ....and the Lord's bondservant must not be quarrelsome, but be kind to all, able to teach, patient when wronged, with gentleness correcting those who are in opposition, if perhaps God may grant them repentance leading to the knowledge of the truth [Gal. 6:1-2; 2 Tim. 2:24-26].

When confronting others it is best if we tell them we oppose their sin primarily because we care for them and do not wish them harm by their continued sin. Severe criticism is more appropriate for those leading others astray. This seems to be Jesus' pattern. He was gentle to sinners, but tough on those leading others astray. We cannot expect others to be perfect.

• For we all stumble in many ways. If anyone does not stumble in what he says, he is a perfect man, able to bridle the whole body as well....Therefore let him who thinks he stands take heed lest he fall...[James 3:2; 1 Cor. 10:12].

Regardless of whether one endures another's unreasonable expectations or confronts a critic, one might have to give up trying to please everyone. God's approval is all that matters.

6. *Cause for Depression*; False doctrine. Counsel for depression: truth.

Often depression comes from a false world-view or false doctrines. One could argue this belongs in the sinful category. If one hears the truth and rejects it, then depression arising from false doctrine would indeed be a sin. However, many are led astray by false teachers and honestly do not know the truth. They do not realize the connection between poor false teaching and depressed feelings. Sometimes the situation is less a matter of rebellion than a matter of being deceived.

Paul links shaken composure of mind with false doctrine.

• Now we request you, brethren, with regard to the coming of our Lord Jesus Christ, and our gathering together to Him, that you may not be **quickly shaken from your composure or be disturbed either by a spirit or a message or a letter as if**

from us, to the effect that the day of the Lord has come [2 Thess. 2:1-2].

• If we have hoped in Christ in this life only, we are of all men most to be pitied [1 Cor. 15:19].

It probably is not possible for an unsaved person to avoid depression. Evolution, atheism, the denial of life after death, working to earn salvation, are all depressive. The Thessalonians were disturbed in spirit by false doctrine on end-time events. Some forms of theology invite depression in those not healed, not rich, or not constantly excited.

Most people have a distorted view of God. They have either been given a false view of God from their religion or they might transfer the traits of an imperfect father-figure from their past over to God. They might also create their own image of what God is like. The true God is holy but gracious. True doctrine is that all are made in God's image. God loves all enough to sacrifice His Son as payment for sin. **God graciously gives eternal life to all who trust in His Son, the Lord Jesus Christ, as Savior.**

• For God so loved the world that He gave His only begotten Son, that **whosoever believes in Him** should not perish, but have eternal life [John 3:16].

Good theology produces good psychology.

7. *Cause for Depression*; Loneliness. Counsel for such depression: fellowship with God and people.

Yet another factor in Elijah's depression was loneliness. "...**I alone am left**; and they seek my life..."(1 Kings 19:10). Elijah felt alone and was depressed. In reality he was not alone. Neither are we. It is hard to overemphasize the need for fellowship in a local church and for Christians to encourage one another.

• (N)ot forsaking our own assembling together, as is the habit of some, but encouraging one another, and all the more, as you see the day drawing near [Heb. 10:25].

In addition to human companionship, God is our ultimate friend.

• Let your character be free from the love of money… for He Himself has said, "I will never desert you, nor will I ever forsake you," so that we may confidently say, "the Lord is my Helper, I will not be afraid, what shall man do to me?" [Heb. 13:5,6].

8. *Cause for Depression*; Medical depression (exhaustion, "burnout," or physical infirmity). Counsel for depression: rest, healthy lifestyle, medicine.

Exhaustion was a primary factor in Elijah's depression. Rather than giving counsel, the angel of the Lord told Elijah to eat and then let him rest. "Arise, eat, because **the journey is too great for you**…" (1 Kings 19:7). Psalm 102 gives the prayer of a sick person. Verse four says, "My heart has been smitten… and has withered away." Exhaustion, sickness, even "the cabin fever" feeling of confinement over a long winter, and burnout, do affect emotions. While secularists might overemphasize biological factors and be hasty to prescribe medicine, Christians should not rule out medical aspects in depression. A conservative approach to using medicine for depression is wise, but a rejection of even the possibility of medicine is not. Some depression is medical in origin. Other times the depression may have begun with purely spiritual and/or emotional needs but has also led to medical problems, for example, potential suicide, sleeplessness, or eating disorders. In cases of serious suicide risk, the immediate attention should be upon survival, not painstaking diagnosis of the exact causes of depression. Even suicidal depression that ultimately turns out to have many non-medical factors often needs medical supervision until the person possesses a more controlled mind capable of pastoral counseling. The hospital, not the church, is the place for around-the-clock supervision to prevent suicide. After a day or two of calm, rest, and "suicide watch", the person may be better able to consider the Biblical remedies for depression referred to above.

Most of the time complaints about depression do not involve suicide risk. Then a counselor may begin by evaluating the spiritual/emotional needs that have been listed in this study. If these spiritual/emotional factors in depression can be ruled out and one tries a healthy lifestyle without alleviation of depression, then medicine may well be necessary. However, even when necessary, medicine alone is never sufficient. The "abundant life" begins by **faith in the Lord Jesus Christ as Savior.**

• The thief comes only to steal, and kill, and destroy; I came that they might have life, and might have in abundantly [John 10:10].

We all need to focus on a perfect God as the source for meaning and satisfaction not self or a seriously flawed world full of disappointing people and things. Failure to do so means we will remain depressed with or without medicine.

Summary:

The Bible gives much insight into the causes and cures for depression. The above 19 factors may also be divided into four larger groupings: depression from sin, depression from being the victim of sin, depression from false world-views or false doctrine, and depression from medical problems such as exhaustion or sickness. We might begin by asking a depressed person to consider all non-medical factors that might be the cause of his or her depression. They usually can identify one or more problems in life. Next, probe for a healthy lifestyle and ask about exhaustion. Sometimes rest...

• And he lay down and slept under a juniper tree; and behold, there was an angel touching him...so he ate and drank and lay down again...[1 Kings 19:5a, 6b].

...comedy...

• A joyful heart is good medicine, but a broken spirit dries up the bones [Prov. 17:22].

... music...

• Let our lord now command your servants who are before you. Let them seek a man who is a skillful player on the harp; and it shall come about when the evil spirit from God is upon you, that he shall play the harp with his hand, and you will be well [1 Sam. 16:16,23].

...and substitution of bad thoughts for good...

• Finally, brethren, whatever is true, whatever is honorable, whatever is right, whatever is pure, whatever is lovely, whatever is of good repute, if there is any excellence and if anything worthy of praise, let your mind dwell upon these things. The things you have learned and received and heard and seen in me, practice these things, and the God of peace shall be with you [Phil. 4:8-9].

... may help with depression. If all the previous spiritual, emotional, and relational factors are ruled out and one remains depressed, then medical advice would be appropriate. Christians using prescriptions for depression should not feel false guilt, but they should understand that those who need medicine still need the teaching of God's Word about our emotions.

A Sermon on Jonah
An Example of Depression from Scripture

The Pouting Prophet

If the Book of Jonah were pure fiction it would end with Chapter three, because you have Jonah delivered; he goes to Nineveh and it's a great revival and everyone lives happily ever after. That is the way you would write a book of fiction, with everybody living happily ever after. But the Bible is history and it records what actually happened, so it shows all of humanity's failures. And God wants to include the heart and mind of Jonah because after the revival he is a first rate mess, and he has a bad attitude, that being true to human nature and that being true to the actual facts that are recorded in Jonah Chapter 4. I decided to preach this sermon backwards, so what we will do is we'll read Jonah Chapter 4. Then we will talk about Jonah's main characteristic here, which is depression. Please turn to Jonah Chapter 4, and we'll look at Jonah's attitude. What you have here if you are looking for a title is *The Pouting Prophet*. Expanded, we might call it *The Pouting Prophet and A Patient God*. We will begin with the close of the story of Jonah, and then take up his main character trait here, which is depression.

• But it greatly displeased Jonah and he became angry [Jonah 4:1].

What really displeased Jonah was the fact that God did not destroy Nineveh and that Nineveh had a great revival. It made him mad. Verse 2:

• [A]nd he prayed to the Lord and said, "please Lord, was not this what I said while I was still in my own country? Therefore, in order to forestall this I fled from Tarshish, for I knew that Thou art a gracious and compassionate God, slow to anger and abundant in lovingkindness, and one who relents concerning calamity. Therefore now, O Lord, please take my life from me, for death is better to me than life [Jonah 4:2-3].

Note that he's also suicidal. We can consider that depressed. Verse 4:

• And the Lord said, "do you have good reason to be angry?" [Jonah 4:4].

Jonah never answers that one. Verse 5:

• Then Jonah went out from the city and sat east of it. There he made a shelter for himself and sat under it in the shade until he could see what would happen in the city. So the Lord God appointed a plant and it grew up over Jonah to be a shade over his head to deliver him from his discomfort. And Jonah was extremely happy about the plant. But God appointed a worm when dawn came the next day, and it attacked the plant and it withered. And it came about that when the sun came up that God appointed a scorching east wind, and the sun beat down on Jonah's head so that he became faint and begged with all his soul to die, saying, "death is better to me than life" [Jonah 4:5-8].

And, he's depressed. Verse 9:

• Then God said to Jonah "do you have good reason to be angry about the plant?" And he said, "I have good reason to be angry, even to death." Then the Lord said, "you had compassion upon the plant for which you did not work, and which you did not cause to grow, which came up overnight and perished overnight. And should not I have compassion on

Nineveh, the great city in which there are more than 120,000 persons who do not know the difference between their right and left hand, as well as many animals? [Jonah 4:9-11].

In other words, there are 120,000 little children in this city, and you, Jonah, care more about a plant than you do them. You are really, really upset that the plant died, and you don't care if the whole city is dying and perishing spiritually. But you care about this insignificant plant dying.

There is a deliberate contrast between Chapter 3 and Chapter 4. **God is no longer angry at Nineveh. He has forgiven them.** And Jonah is angry that God has forgiven them. God has compassion and mercy, and Jonah is angry. He cares more about a plant than he does the whole city. There are all kinds of examples in the Bible of people who are depressed to the point of being suicidal. Those are the sections that you would go to if you wanted to develop what the Bible teaches about depression. It is obvious to say that if somebody wants to die they're depressed, and so you look at their stories and you analyze them, and you see what causes and what cures there are for such depression.

First of all, some people definitely need medicine. But the other thing about it is that in a secular system where man is nothing more than a animal and everything is biological, everything gets lumped into one category. People who think they can fix everything by medicine are deluding themselves. Those that practice that way aren't helping people. They mask the problems, they simply numb them for a while and the depressed never do get better. Therefore, both extremes are true; some people definitely need medicine for depression. Many others, medicine won't help. Depression is really not that complex of a topic. We're going to be able to deal with it here in 20-25 minutes and pretty much have the gist of the Bible's answers on depression. But it's not totally simplistic

either. You have to think about it a little bit. You have to think
about the possible causes of depression, and when you reverse
these causes you will find that the Bible has answers for them.
So let's give some ideas on depression.

The first thing I'd like to say is that a certain amount of
depression that we might call the "blues", is normal. Let's look
at Romans 8. We'll go away from the story from Jonah for a
few seconds, and we'll read Romans 8, verse 22. We want to
glance at the context before and after.

• For we know that the whole creation groans and suffers the
pains of childbirth together until now [Rom. 8:22].

Basically what Paul is saying in the context is that it is
a cursed world. Now I think there can be such a thing as joy,
but joy isn't dependent upon emotion, joy is satisfaction with
God regardless of the circumstances. So we can be satisfied
with God even when everything in life is not going very well.
We can have joy. But being happy and giddy all the time is
kind of unrealistic. Some people think you have to be walking
on cloud nine all the time, that everything has to be so
wonderful every day. That's not my experience, and I don't
think it's realistic to expect that because this verse is telling us
that the *whole creation* groans and travails in pain. There is
going to be joy, but it's not going to *always* be good, and there
are going to be days when the alarm clock goes off really early,
and we're going to say to ourselves I wish I didn't have to get
out of bed and work and earn my bread with the sweat of my
brow. Expecting to live on a high plain of happiness and
euphoria and giddiness all the time doesn't work. I know better
than that. If the alarm clock goes off, it's all right if we say we
don't want to get up at 4 o'clock and go milk the cows, but
when we can no longer go to work, we don't eat or we eat too
much, or we sleep all the time, or we never sleep all night, then
it's a more serious level of depression. That can happen too,

and that is a different problem. But to expect to feel euphoria all the time is unrealistic.

The next thing I want to say is a victim of sin can become depressed. In seminary we had this world-famous teacher. In his books he said depression is always sin. The first thing that came to mind when I read this was the Garden of Gethsemane, and if Jesus wasn't feeling discouraged or depressed in the Garden of Gethsemane, then I guess I don't know the definition of what depression is. Jesus didn't sin. Jesus was the victim of sin. He felt the oppression of all the darkness of the sins of the human race lying on His shoulders, and it bothered Him. Let's review that one, Matthew 26:38 will be where we will look.

• Then he said to them, "My soul is deeply grieved to the point of death; remain here and keep watch with Me. And he went a little beyond them, and fell on His face and prayed, saying, "My Father, if it is possible, let this cup pass from Me, yet not as I will, but as Thou wilt" [Matt. 26:38].

We have probably different definitions and thoughts for depression, but I don't know what else this is but some type or level of depression. Jesus wasn't a sinner. It wasn't due to His own fault in this case. He was the victim of other people's wrongdoings inflicted upon Him. When that happens, we have to be careful that we turn our problems over to God (when we've been victimized by sin) because if we don't draw closer to God, then we will respond with sins of our own. It's very easy to be innocent and be the victim of another's sin, then to respond with sins of our own. Being cheated, or being betrayed, or being the victim of sin in itself is not a sin, but I do think it can lead to depression. It depends on how we handle it. Jesus did the right thing; He went to the Father with it. There was no sin on His part, but He was having a difficult time here.

We can give some suggestions on how to help other people with, or help ourselves with, this type of depression when we've been wronged. Hebrews 10 talks about *not forsaking the assembling of yourselves together*, and encouraging one another so much the more as you see "the day drawing near". It's pretty hard to go overboard on encouragement. Very hard. The brothers and sisters in Christ need encouragement. It's a habit that all of us ought to try to cultivate because other people constantly have pressures on them, and part of the fellowship in the body of Christ is encouraging one another.

Our own thought processes and meditation also help with depression. We won't read Philippians 4 right here, but that's where it says be anxious for nothing but in everything with prayer and supplication with thanksgiving let your requests be known unto God. In other words, in your thinking you substitute all that worry and all that depression with prayers and Bible verses. Then the context goes on to say whatever is lovely, whatever is virtuous, whatever is of good report, think on these things. We can substitute the awful thoughts for the good thoughts by turning to Scripture and turning to the Person of God in prayer. I also believe that Saul's example in the Old Testament shows that music can be a help with depression. Saul had terrible depression, his was a sinful depression, it came out of jealousy, he was jealous of David. That's where his depression came from. But music was of some help in alleviating that, and I am a believer in Christian music. It's not so much the emotion of the music, it's the ideas, the truth in the music to which we respond with emotions. It's not music in general that I think can help with depression, but rather the truths expressed in good Christian music. When these are presented in an emotionally appealing way it can be helpful.

Let's move on now to make room for the idea that depression can be of medical origin. I don't think it's 100% of the cases. It's very poor practice to leave people the idea that all types of depression can be fixed with medicine. That's not true. Medicine masks much of it. Some people need it, and we'll include that here in a second. Elijah is a case where he needed a little bit of better health, that's First Kings 19. We haven't time to give the whole story of Elijah here, but what happened was the prophet confronted the prophets of Baal on the mountain. He won the battle, and you would have thought that my goodness, he ought to be really rejoicing and happy. He confronted the prophets of Baal and he won. But sometimes the battle is very stressful. Sometimes you just get worn out in the battle. Whatever type of battle it is, you just get exhausted when it's all done. And that's what happened to Elijah, he was just all worn out. Jezebel wanted to kill him and he ran and he ran and he ran and he went to a remote place, and he was totally exhausted. Let's look at this in First Kings 19, verse 4.

• But he himself went a day's journey into the wilderness, and came and sat down under a juniper tree; and he requested for himself that he might die, and said, "it is enough; now, O Lord, take my life, for I am not better than my fathers" [1 Kings 19:4].

So you see, he is depressed, he is suicidal. And he's all worn out from running away from Jezebel. Here is how God helps him. Verse five:

• And he lay down and slept under a juniper tree; and behold, there was an angel touching him, and he said to him, "arise, eat." Then he looked and behold, there was at his head a bread cake baked on hot stones, and a jar of water. So he ate and drank and lay down again. And the angel of the Lord came a second time and touched him and said, "arise, eat, because **the journey is too great for you**" [1 Kings 19:5-7].

Here is a main reason for Elijah's depression;

•...the journey is too great for you [1 Kings 19:7].

So God comes to him and gives him intensive psychotherapy, right? Here's all this advice. Or He comes to him and gives him all this theology, right? No, what God says is you're all worn out Elijah, eat this meal and rest a while. There's God's first step for help for Elijah's depression, because his depression comes from just sheer exhaustion. Am I the only one who gets depressed and crabby when he's worn out? I can't be. We all do. Depression can be this simple. God tells Elijah, "you are burned out". We get tired. Then we get discouraged, and finally get depressed. We get mad at everything. That's the way it happens. And in this case the first thing was, "practice sensible living Elijah, get caught up, take a vacation, take a break, here's the food, here's the rest", and I think that a lot of times that when depression is medical in origin, step one is rest.

Now if that doesn't work, maybe we do need medicine. Fine. Some people do. Because there are so many people in the world we can say many people do need medicine for their depression. But it's not for everybody. It's not even the majority. Many people, where the depression is of medical origin, are just plain worn out. It's unrealistic to try to do too much. Then they become like Elijah, they crash in a heap, "oh I want to die, want to die", and there are probably times in our lives where everybody gets to that point, and it can simply be just because they're worn out.

There is a way to sensibly approach it. If we just can't shake depression we ought to first examine our lives and find out if there is sin there. If there is no sin there (and we have a good idea of what's right and wrong), then we ought to see if we have been living carefully as far as our general health routine. Do we sleep, do we eat right, are we all worn out? After those things are tried, if we still can't shake it, then maybe we need medicine. That's okay. But medicine is not the first thing we try. Try other things first. And if we need medicine (some in our church may, maybe some day I might), that doesn't mean we don't need God. We need to do both. Those who do need the medicine also may need to work on their spirituality and work on their walk with God.

So we see that Elijah is a case where depression can be medical in origin. I do want to add this, however. Sometimes it can be backwards. A person can start out with a real spiritual problem in his or her life, and it becomes a physical problem. It can go that direction. The underlying cause is really spiritual, but it eats on him so much it affects his health. A person in that situation needs both medical help and spiritual help. I believe alcoholism is another case where there is that pattern. A person who is an alcoholic needs both need medical and spiritual help. It may start out as a spiritual problem, but now it's also a medical problem. Now it's both.

There are other examples of people in the Bible who wanted to die. We will look at the reasons why they were depressed. Come with me to Psalm 51 please. David is writing here; in his case he is depressed because he is guilty. He ought to be. He stole another man's wife. Then he killed him. And he ought to feel depressed, but in his case it is the guilt that is causing depression. And so in Psalm 51 he is confessing that guilt so as to be restored.

• [W]ash me thoroughly from my iniquity, and cleanse me from my sin. For I know my transgressions, and my sin is ever before me [Psa. 51:2-3].

It's eating on me and it's bugging me, and I'm depressed. Now look at Psalm 51, verse 12 where he confesses his sin,

• Restore to me the joy of Thy salvation [Psa. 51:12].

In other words, I'd like my peace of mind back. I'd like my happiness back. I'd like to get over this depression. In David's problem, it is his guilt. Guilt is a legitimate cause of depression. People have sinned, and it bothers their conscience. That's a good thing, actually, because it tells them they ought to do something about their sin. They ought to get a spiritual remedy for it. I believe that a lot of Americans are depressed because of guilt, and they haven't dealt with it rightly, and a pill won't fix it. I'll make room for the medical part of it, and the exhaustion part of it, but there are a lot of Americans that are not in that bad of health, and yet they are depressed because of their guilt. They haven't brought it to the cross. They're going to feel guilty and depressed, and it's not going to go away.

False guilt is also a cause of depression. Let me quote First John 3:20 to you:

• [I]n whatever our heart condemn us, for God is greater than our heart, and knoweth all things [1 John 3:20, KJV].

"If our heart condemns us, God is greater than our heart and knows all things." In other words, there are some things for which we feel guilt, but God knows it was an accident or wasn't our fault, or really wasn't even Biblically wrong. We just think it was wrong because we haven't been trained correctly, or we got bad teaching somewhere along the line, and we feel guilty about it. For instance, say you have a car accident and you hurt somebody. You didn't really mean to harm another, but you feel so guilty about it, and you can't shake it. Or you have to put mother in the nursing home, and it just bothers you, and there's this terrible guilt. These types of false guilt can cause depression too. We really didn't do anything wrong, but we have the feelings. This verse says God is greater than our hearts and knows all things. We will not turn again to Elijah's example, but addition to being exhausted Elijah is lonely. We know this because he said,

• ...I alone am left... [1 Kings 19:10].

I'm the only one left! And then the answer was, well, there's at least 7,000 other people that have not bowed their knees to Baal! But when people are really lonely, they tend to get depressed. And here they need other people to help them if they are severely depressed. Someone needs to show kindness and friendship, or, perhaps they need to show the initiative to work harder at building friends. But loneliness causes it. Loneliness causes depression.

Let's look at the next two examples at the same time; we'll look at Numbers 11, and First Kings 21. The first concerns Moses, Numbers 11, and verse 10. Everybody's complaining about Moses. They say, "Moses is a bummer of a leader". Numbers 11 verse 10:

• Now Moses heard the people weeping throughout their families, each man at the doorway of his tent; and the anger of the Lord was kindled greatly, and Moses was displeased. So Moses said to the LORD, "why hast Thou been so hard on Thy servant? And why have I not found favor in Thy sight, that Thou have laid the burden of all this people on me?" [Num. 11:10-11].

Who made me their leader? I don't want to be their leader anymore. Who put me here? Verse 12:

• Was it I who conceived all this people? Was it I who brought them forth, that Thou shouldst say to me, "carry them in your bosom as a nurse carries a nursing infant, to the land which Thou didst swear to your fathers?" Where am I going to get meat (food) to give all this people? For they weep before me saying, "give us meat that we may eat". I alone am not able to carry all this people, because it is to burdensome for me. So if Thou art going to deal thus with me, please kill me at once… [Num. 11:12-15a].

So God, if you're going to deal this way with me please kill me at once. There are a number of different ways to express his problem here. First, he is depressed, and he is suicidal. Moses really feels like the responsibility for the whole world is on his shoulders, and he can't handle it. Well, nobody can. Probably people in this type of church tend to be perfectionists because we're all serious people. That's why we come here to study the Bible in every little detail. We tend to be that way. We do want to live life with excellence, but there are a lot of things we can't fix. We cannot control them. But maybe God didn't make me the savior of the world. Maybe he didn't make you the savior of the world either. We do what we can do, but we're not messiahs. Moses wasn't God either. He couldn't control all these millions of Jewish people who were constantly hounding him and never happy. He couldn't fix it. There are some redeeming qualities about being a perfectionist; usually things get done with excellence and that's good. But one of the casualties of it may be depression. The cure here is realizing ones limitations and turning it over to God. We can't fix everything. We can't do everything. We can't change everybody.

Next, greed can be a cause of depression. Ahab is an example of greed. These people are interesting when you can be detached and stand back and look at their stories. It is interesting to watch human nature in Bible stories. In First

Kings 21, Ahab wants his neighbor's vineyard. I have driven by this spot in Israel, and when everything is green, you could look at this place and you could see why somebody would want it. So Ahab wants this field, but his neighbor won't sell it to him. Let's look at how he responds:

• So Ahab came into his house sullen and vexed because of the word which Naboth the Jezreelite had spoken to him; for he said, "I will not give you the inheritance of my fathers." And he lay down on his bed and turned away his face and ate no food. But Jezebel his wife came to him and said to him, "How is it that your spirit is so sullen that you are not eating food?" [1 Kings 21:4].

In other words I can't have it. I can't have what I want. He had much money but he couldn't have what he wanted. He's really depressed, because he wants something badly, and he cannot have it. We are constantly bombarded with advertisements to make us discontent. Because we need to have more, and if we'll just buy things we'll be happy. There's an appropriate story about a factory in Brazil. A manufacturer built a factory because of low wages in the country. They paid these people a low wage thinking this is great; we'll ship the product back to America, and sell it for huge profit. After the first paycheck people quit working. Their attitude was we have all the money we need. We got a paycheck; it will last us for a long time. We don't need to work anymore. So these people that planned this factory had a problem on their hands because of the mindset of the people. Because they didn't feel consumerism, they didn't feel the need to work every week or to work until they dropped so they could buy more. They wondered, "how are we going to fix this?". They'll work for nothing, but they won't work for long. So they imported a whole bunch of catalogs of merchandise. Thus, they upped the level of the worker's needs, and they got them to work just like we work. Till we drop. We must watch the greed and consumerism. We all like nice things, but we cannot get depressed, because everybody has limits. Can't have this car. Can't have these clothes. Can't have this house. It's never going to happen. So we can either live with it and be content with God, or we can get depressed, and we can stay depressed. So greed is one of the causes of depression.

Fear is another cause of depression; Psalm 42 verse 5:

• Why are you in despair, O my soul....hope in God...[Psa. 42:5].

Jealousy. Saul was jealous of David. He is the most depressed character in the Bible. Saul went out and heard, "Saul has killed his thousands, but David his ten thousands." It is kind of Jonah's problem too, he hates, he has anger. He hates Nineveh, but they're being blessed. If we hate somebody, really hate them, but life is good with them, we get depressed. *We don't hurt them any either.* By the way, they usually don't care about our jealousy. They probably don't even know about it. So we have depression from jealousy.

False teaching also depresses people. The example of this is in Second Thessalonians chapter two. What's happening here is that people have taught the Thessalonians that they're in the Tribulation period. It wasn't true. But just being taught that they were in the Tribulation really bothered them.

• Now we request you, brethren, with regard to the coming of our Lord Jesus Christ, and our gathering together to Him, that you may not be quickly shaken from your composure or be disturbed either by a spirit or a message or a letter as if from us, to the effect that the Day of the Lord has come [2 Thess. 2: 1-2].

The Thessalonians got some false teaching. They're all worried about it. They thought they were in the Tribulation and that the antichrist was going to come and persecute them. False teaching will do that. The number one category of false teaching that depresses people is evolution. All kinds of false doctrine depress people. One day the state government sent somebody over here for counseling because they were confused about Bible doctrine. The state government determined that they could not help them. This was a theological problem. Their church confused them. There is such a thing as theological malpractice. False doctrine can really hurt people. Certain false doctrines are really destructive. One of the side effects of false doctrine is depression.

Now we have to tie this all together in some way. Sometimes depression is medical in origin. Other times it's sinful. I think the thing to do is to examine the heart. Above all, we must choose to trust in the Lord Jesus Christ as Savior letting His substitute death on the cross be the payment for our sin. After faith in Christ, we are *forgiven* before God as *Judge* and will go to heaven. Yet, we must still confess sins to obtain forgiveness before God as *Father* to *remain in fellowship* with God.

If we don't have any unconfessed sin, then we go on to consider non-sinful causes of depression. We might try sensible living, maybe we're exhausted. If that doesn't work, maybe we need medicine. Depression might arise from sin or being the victim of sin, or false doctrine, or from poor health. The Bible gives us wisdom for the causes for our depression and wisdom for the cure of such depression.

Let's pray together.

DEMONS
OR
MENTAL ILLNESS?

How does one diagnose
demon possession? What factors
differentiate demon possession
from mental illness? What implied
strategies would a Christian worker
employ if one encounters
demon influence?

This research arose from the author's ministry to families of the mentally ill.
Christian leaders from diverse denominations from around the world asked
for suggestions as to differentiate the demonic from the psychiatric.

DEMONS
OR
MENTAL ILLNESS

Dr. Steven Waterhouse

Dangers of Diagnosis

In some theological circles demon influence seems to be a frequent and convenient diagnosis to explain most sins or any odd behavior. By contrast, scholarly researchers agree on the need for great caution in diagnosing demon possession. Even those who disagree on specifics completely agree the diagnosing of demons is a serious matter.

"One can also see how much damage can be done by well meaning exorcists who, by the very act of exorcism, suggest to the counselee that demons are present. If the "exorcism" fails, the counselee is left not only with his original symptoms but with hopelessness and despair because he thinks his body is possessed by stubborn demons who refuse to leave".[1]

"Unless there are non-pathological symptoms such as magical healing powers, speaking in languages not learned, clairvoyance, and so on, we must not presume the demonic".[2]

---

[1] *Gary R. Collins, "Psychological Observations on Demonology", in* Demon Possession, *ed., John Warwick Montgomery (Minneapolis: Bethany House Publishers, 1976), 246.*

[2] C. Fred Dickason, *Demon Possession and the Christian* (Westchester: Crossway Books, 1987), 327.

"Never in my life have I ever said to a person, 'You are demon possessed', even on the occasions when I have actually felt this to be the case. We have no right whatsoever to confront a person with so grave a diagnosis as this. At most one can form a prayer group for the person, telling those who take part that the symptoms point to a possible case of possession....we can pray for a person without having to say what we think is wrong with him." [3]

"...how easy it is to arrive at a false diagnosis if one fails to exercise sufficient care when seeking to assess the demonic. One must be especially careful in this area, for the distinguishing between disease and the demonic is not only a very difficult task but also a very responsible one....Unfortunately there are many Christians who are all too ready to accept the presence of the demonic in doubtful cases of emotional disturbance....If such a person is told glibly that Satan has bound him or even possessed him, this reproach can itself lead to much restlessness, fear, and depression in the patient....I have witnessed on numerous occasions the adverse effects produced on emotionally ill people when they have been incorrectly diagnosed as suffering from demonic subjection. To further burden a person suffering from mental illness by telling him that he has fallen into the hands of the devil is inexcusable. Anyone who voices an opinion of this nature without having any knowledge of abnormal mental behaviour is not only acting very rashly but may also be subjecting the patient to an untold amount of cruelty." [4]

"The New Testament accounts never picture 'secret' demonization! People were assumed to be free from demons

---

[3] Kurt Koch and Alfred Lechler, *Occult Bondage and Deliverance*, reprint ed. (Grand Rapids: Kregal, 1971), 64.
[4] Ibid., 188-189.

unless they displayed the obvious symptoms of possession mentioned earlier." [5]

The literature on this subject gives some pathetic examples of the misdiagnosis of demon possession. One poor woman with terminal cancer was told the real problem was that her mother was demon-possessed.[6] Another young lady with mental problems was first told that the voices she heard were from the Holy Spirit. Then the same group said her voices were demonic. All she really needed was proper medication. [7]

Asserting the need for caution and wisdom in the area of diagnosing demon possession is not saying that a probable diagnosis need be so difficult as to be impossible. Many authors make the correct observation that people of New Testament times had no trouble agreeing about cases of demon possession. Demon possession was so unique as to be obvious. Whether Jesus or the apostles or the Jewish leaders or the common people, all seemed to recognize demon possession when they saw it.

"No one in the New Testament ever disagreed about the presence of demons in a specific case of possession ....Everyone, believers and unbelievers alike, seemed just to know." [8]

---

[5] Alex Konya, *Demons: A Biblically Based Perspective* (Schaumburg: Regular Baptist Press, 1990), 32.

[6] W. Elwyn Davies, "Demonology and Pastoral Care," in *Demon Possession*, 304.

[7] James D. Mallory, Jr., "Response," in *Demon Possession*, 322.

[8] John White, "Problems and Procedures in Exorcism," in *Demon Possession*, 282.

"When these accounts are carefully examined, one finds that true demonic possession was so terrible and extreme that people had little difficulty identifying it for what it was." [9]

"There is no indication that specialists were used to diagnose demon possession. In fact, the diagnosis of demon possession does not seem to have been a problem." [10]

There is need for warnings about casual diagnoses of demon possession. On a mission trip to Africa the author met a Kenyan who was convinced his daughter was being seized by demons in the middle of the night. The real problem was simply sleep apnea. A flippant misdiagnosis in such situations caused a family deep pain. Ugandan pastors also testified they encountered naked people in trees crying and shouting. Believing them to be demon-possessed the pastors drove them deeper into the jungle (where they probably perished from starvation or wild animals). A final diagnosis of demon possession may even be correct in this situation. Yet, it is just as likely these poor people needed psychiatric help. By dismissing this possibility from the outset and rushing to the conclusion of demon possession, pastoral care can lead to disastrous results. It is even better to plead ignorance than give a casual and hasty diagnosis. Suicide prevention and medical care would have been in order regardless of the true nature of the problem.

One is on much safer grounds to reserve the possibility for demonic involvement only in those cases that parallel New Testament symptoms. Of course, the greater number of

---

[9] Alex Konya, *Demons: A Biblically Based Perspective*, 19-20.
[10] Willem Berends, "The Biblical Criteria For Demon Possession," *Westminster Theological Journal* 37(3) (1975), 352.

symptoms which exist the greater confidence there could be in a diagnosis.

The following material lists Biblical characteristics of demon possession, and then discusses differences between possession and mental illness.

Biblical Characteristics of Demon Possession

The New Testament records many symptoms of demon possession. Any consideration of demonic control should begin with an evaluation of a person by a list of the Biblical facts about demon possession.

Alterations in Voice

Demons would speak through the body of a possessed person. They would claim to be separate from the person (Luke 4:33-34).

• "[A]nd shouting out with a loud voice, he said, 'What business do we have to do with each other, Jesus, Son of the Most High God? I implore You by God, do not torment me!' For He had been saying to him, 'Come out of the man, you unclean spirit!' And He was asking him, 'What is your name?' And he said to Him, 'My name is Legion; for we are many' " [Mark 5:7-9].

Supernatural Knowledge

Demons knew information about end time punishment. Demon-possessed people could identify Jesus Christ before they were introduced to Him. They even knew the true identity of Christ before the disciples did! (Matt. 8:29; Mark 1:24, 5:7; Luke 4:34, 8:28; Acts 16:16-18).

• "[S]aying, 'What business do we have with each other, Jesus of Nazareth? Have You come to destroy us? I know who You are - the Holy One of God!' [Mark 1:24]. (Peter finally understands Christ's complete identity seven chapters later in Mark 8:29).

• "And it happened that as we were going to the place of prayer, a certain slave-girl having a spirit of divination met us, who was bringing her masters much profit by fortunetelling. Following after Paul and us, she kept crying out, saying, 'These men are bond-servants of the Most High God, who are proclaiming to you the way of salvation' " [Acts 16:16-17].

Superhuman Strength

Demon-possessed people could block a road or tear away chains. They terrified others with feats of strength.

• "And when He had come to the other side into the country of the Gadarenes, two men who were demon-possessed met Him...They were so exceedingly violent that no one could pass by that road" [Matt. 8:28].

• "When He got out of the boat, immediately a man from the tombs with an unclean spirit met Him, and he had his dwelling among the tombs. And no one was able to bind him anymore, even with a chain; because he had often been bound with shackles and chains, and the chains had been torn apart by him, and the shackles broken in pieces, and no one was strong enough to subdue him" [Mark 5:2-4].

• "And the man, in whom was the evil spirit, leaped on them and subdued all of them and overpowered them, so that they fled out of that house naked and wounded" [Acts 19:16].

Uncleanness

Would not a desire to live in a cemetery coupled with nudity suggest an interest in unclean things?

• "And when He had come out onto the land, He was met by a man from the city who was possessed with demons; and who had not put on any clothing for a long time, and was not living in a house, but in the tombs" [Luke 8:27, see also Mark 5:2-3].

Physiological Complications

Demonic control over a body can extend to eyes, ears, and voice box. Obviously, there must also be other factors present or these should be considered natural medical ailments.

• "Then a demon-possessed man who was blind and mute was brought to Jesus, and He healed him, so that the mute man spoke and saw" [Matt. 12:22].

• "When Jesus saw that a crowd was rapidly gathering, He rebuked the unclean spirit, saying to it, 'You deaf and mute spirit, I command you, come out of him and do not enter him again' " [Mark 9:25].

• "And He was casting out a demon, and it was mute; when the demon had gone out, the mute man spoke; and the crowds were amazed" [Luke 11:14].

Suicidal Tendencies

In the New Testament it was not uncommon for demoniacs to exhibit self-destructive behavior.

• "Lord, have mercy on my son, for he is a lunatic and is very ill; for he often falls into the fire, and often into the water.... And Jesus rebuked him, and the demon came out of him, and the boy was cured at once" [Matt. 17:15,18].

• "Constantly, night and day, he was screaming among the tombs and in the mountains, and gashing himself with stones" [Mark 5:5].

Recognition of Christ's Authority Coupled with Resistance to Spiritual Things

There seems to have been a "push-pull" relationship between Christ and demons. They spoke to the Lord with respect. One demon-possessed man even ran to worship Him. However, at the same time the demons did not want to be around Christ. It seems as if they were under a compulsion to acknowledge His authority, but their true feelings were hatred and fear. Despite being forced to worship against their will, they really wanted no dealings whatsoever with the Lord Jesus Christ. There are several situations where demons express their aversion to Christ but do so with respectful words (Matt. 8:29; Mark 1:24; Luke 4:34, 8:27-28).

• "Seeing Jesus from a distance, he ran up and bowed down before Him; and shouting with a loud voice, he said, 'What business do we have with each other, Jesus, Son of the Most High God...?' " [Mark 5:6, 7]

Many authors believe that a demon-possessed person will not come voluntarily for help. Their opinion is that those who claim to be demon-possessed are probably drawing attention to themselves (or have been deceived by ignorant counsel) whereas the truly possessed will try to withdraw from contact with Christianity unless it is unavoidable. Typically, a demon-possessed individual was brought to Christ by others, or Christ was in the area and could not be easily avoided. After there was contact with the Lord, demons acknowledged His authority even though they did not enjoy His presence.

"We strongly suspect, however, that when a demoniac is confronted with the name and claims of Jesus Christ by one of his followers, he will show some signs of recognition.... we find no instance in which the demoniac came voluntarily and of himself to be cured....We can therefore conclude that in those cases when a person comes to be counseled because he thinks he has a demon, the counselor has every reason to suspect that he is not dealing with a demoniac."[11]

"There is first of all a very simple rule one can adopt. If one meets a person who claims to be demon-possessed, then he is not really demon-possessed. Anyone who is really possessed will neither realize nor broadcast the fact of his possession."[12]

Alfred Lechler directed the largest mental hospital in Germany for 35 years. He agrees with the idea that demoniacs will not willingly come to Christians for help: "...a person who continually talks about being possessed is in fact deluding himself. On the contrary, a person who is really possessed will never let the idea of possession enter his head, even if there is no other explanation for his condition."[13]

---

[11] Willem Berends, "The Biblical Criteria For Demon Possession", *Westminster Theological Journal* 37(3) (1975), 360-361.
[12] Kurt Koch, and Alfred Lechler, *Occult Bondage and Deliverance*, 62.
[13] Ibid., 167.

Prior Interest in Idolatry/Occult

The Bible teaches that demons promote idol worship and use false religion to promote their own works (See Deuteronomy 32:17; Psalm 106:36-38; 1 Corinthians 10:20). Some would apply the principle of sins being passed on to third and fourth generations to the area of occult bondage (Exodus 20:5). Certainly, the demon-possessed girl in Philippi had a prior interest in the occult.

• "It happened that as we were going to the place of prayer, a slave-girl having a spirit of divination met us, who was bringing her masters much profit by fortune telling." [Acts 16:16].

"I have found this avenue of ancestral involvement to be *the chief cause of demonization.* Well over 95 percent of the more than 400 persons I have contacted in my counseling ministry have been demonized because of their ancestor's involvement in occult and demon activities."[14] "I am concerned with individuals presented for assessment and help. In these cases we must always and increasingly be on the alert for any evidence of occult involvement."[15]

Transference or Other Occultic Manifestations

The incident where 2,000 swine ran off the hillside into the Sea of Galilee shows that strange phenomena may accompany demon possession (See Mark 5:13). Other examples of bizarre

---

14 Dickason, C. Fred, *Demon Possession and the Christian*, 221.
15 R. Kenneth McAll, "Taste and See," in *Demon Possession*, 272.

manifestations will surface again in the next section that contrasts possession with mental illness.

Epileptic-like Seizures, Foaming Mouth

This New Testament symptom of demon possession again reinforces the need to have a number of factors converge before one makes any conclusion about the presence of demons. There should be the combination of those factors that go beyond physiological symptoms and involve the additional presence of the supernatural (Matthew 17:15; Mark 1:26, 9:18,26; Luke 4:35, 9:39). Otherwise, those with purely medical problems will be diagnosed foolishly as having demons.

• "Throwing him into convulsions, the unclean spirit cried out with a loud voice and came out of him." [Mark 1:26]

• "[A]nd a spirit seizes him, and he suddenly screams, and it throws him into a convulsion with foaming at the mouth; and only with difficulty does it leave him, mauling him, as it leaves" [Luke 9:39].

The Bible gives some idea as to the symptoms of demon possession. However, some of these same symptoms in isolation can be traced to ordinary medical problems (blindness, muteness, deafness, convulsions). This next section shows that the Bible recognizes the differences between demons and disease. Although demons can cause physical problems, medical problems can obviously arise without them. The most difficult subject is the differentiation between demon possession and mental illness.

Possession vs. Mental Illness

The Bible makes distinctions between diseases and demon possession.

• "...they began bringing to him all who were ill **and** those who were demon-possessed" (Mark 1:32).

Mark 6:13 describes the ministry of the twelve apostles:

• "And they were casting out many demons **and** were anointing with oil many sick people and healing them" [Mark 6:13]. (See also: Matt. 4:24, 9:27-34, 10:1, 8; Mark 1:32,34, 3:10-11, 6:13; Luke 7:21; Acts 5:16, 8:7).

These verses indicate two distinct categories of ailments: disease and demons. Christian counselors who fail to differentiate between brain disorders such as schizophrenia and demon-possession inflict much damage. The argument that mental illnesses such as schizophrenia are valid brain disorders cannot be given here. Although secular psychology/psychiatry can be criticized from the Christian perspective, it is a mistake to ignore all help in the accurate description of human problems. Those who believe the Bible *prescribes* all answers could still benefit from controlled observation of human life that can help *describe* an exact problem. Counseling given without an accurate diagnosis of a person's true problem will not help and could do immense harm.[16] Sometimes even secular researchers argue that possession is an observable

---

[16] Research that attempts to include the existence of mental illness into a framework of a Biblical world view include: Waterhouse, Steven. Strength For His People: A Ministry to the Families of the Mentally Ill. Amarillo: Westcliff, 2002; and Welch, Edward T. Counselor's Guide to the Brain and its Disorders: Knowing the Difference Between Disease and Sin. Grand Rapids: Zondervan, 1991.

phenomenon and that it should be differentiated from known categories of mental illness. Dr. Larry Montz, founder of the International Society for Paranormal Research denies demons attack people. However, he says, "I do believe that possession by entities and ghosts of people who have died is possible."[17]

Whether a secular researcher believes a possession is caused by demons or "ghosts', it remains significant that secular sources can be quoted concluding there is such a thing as possession and that a possessed status cannot be identified with any category of "normal" mental illness.

In a fascinating article, T. Craig Isaacs explains that the purpose of his Ph.D. dissertation was to answer, "is possession a phenomena independent of the current commonly accepted psychodiagnostic categories?"[18] He submitted fourteen cases of those certified as demon-possessed by the Episcopal Church to five experienced psychodiagnosticians. The conclusion was that demon possession is unlike all other categories of mental illness. He was awarded a Ph.D. from The California School of Professional Psychology in Berkeley for his work.

Aversion to Religion vs. Attraction to Religion

Efforts at ministry must take into account the difference between demons and disease, between possession and brain disorders. Six factors seem to distinguish a mental illness such

---

[17] Erik J. Martin, "The Devil Inside: Exorcising the Myth Behind Demonic Possession," in Buffy the Vampire Slayer (Oak Brook: Twentieth Century Fox Film Corporation, Summer 2000), 17. This is a Hollywood publication that promotes a popular television program. The article quoted Vatican officials, paranormal researchers, religious advisors to the production of The Exorcist, and this author.

[18] T. Craig Isaacs, "The Possessive States Disorder: The Diagnosis of Demonic Possession," Pastoral Psychology 35(4) (1987), 264.

as schizophrenia from cases of demon possession described in the New Testament.[19]   Millard Sall, a psychiatrist from Anaheim, California makes this observation:

"Demons want nothing to do with Christ. Conversely, people who are deeply mentally disturbed are often devoutly religious. Unlike demons, they want to be close to Jesus or have some kind of deep religious experience." [20]

Alfred Lechler, a German psychiatrist, reaches the same conclusion. "Furthermore, if he displays no signs of opposition to any form of Christian counseling, or just listens indifferently and remains unmoved where people attempt to exorcise demons, or if he finds no difficulty in pronouncing the name of Jesus all this is indicative of mental illness rather than the demonic." [21]

Many patients in mental hospitals desire religious instruction without initial resistance. By contrast we know from the New Testament that demons hate any involvement

---

[19] Mark 5:15 implies a dual diagnosis where demon possession had affected the host's thinking. Perhaps the "right mind" of Mark 5:15 primarily involved the alleviation of violent and suicidal tendencies. The man definitely had bizarre thinking, but this need not have been identical to schizophrenia or bipolar disorder. Even if Mark 5:15 did involve a diagnosable mental illness caused by demons, the situation would have been similar to other medical problems caused by demons (blindness, muteness, epilepsy). Certainly, most cases of epilepsy do not involve other Biblical indications of demon possession. It is ignorant and cruel to tell those with epilepsy they are demon-possessed. Likewise, most cases of schizophrenia can be differentiated from demon possession as described in the Bible.
[20] Millard J. Sall, "Demon Possession or Psychopathology?: A Clinical Differentiation," *Journal of Psychology and Theology*, 4(4) (1976), 288.
[21] Kurt Koch and Alfred Lechler, *Occult Bondage and Deliverance*, 162.

with the things of Christ. In its ministry to families of the mentally ill, Westcliff Bible Church has experience evangelizing and counseling tens of thousands of those with mental illness. While some of this took place through impersonal means, such as television, radio, and literature, in thousands of cases there is direct and personal counseling or correspondence. Many mentally ill people desire salvation and do submit to the Bible's teachings. This hardly parallels the attitude observed in New Testament cases of demon possession where there is initial aversion to the things of God.

• (A)nd shouting with a loud voice he said, "What business do we have with each other, Jesus, Son of the Most High God?..." [Mark 5:7].

Rational Speech vs. Nonsense

In New Testament accounts demons spoke in a rational manner. They can be quoted in complete sentences with subjects and predicates. Untreated mentally ill people speak in nonsense and jump rapidly between topics.

"The fact that the demons spoke in a rational manner is a third distinction.... They communicated in a logical manner. They were like the devil who spoke clearly with purpose and meaning, possessing the ability to carry on real dialogue. The speech and logical process of the schizophrenic are often incoherent. They produce 'word salads' and irrationalities that do not make sense in contrast to the speech behavior of demons." [22]

"A possessed person is in fact mentally healthy in spite of the fact that at intervals he may exhibit certain symptoms of

---

[22] Millard J. Sall, *Demon Possession or Psychopathology?*, 288.

mental abnormality....Moreover the words the mentally ill person hears are often completely nonsensical." [23]

"In such cases where the voices make sense (not nonsense as in the case of schizophrenia, a condition of chemical imbalance in the brain) ...we should strongly suspect demonic forces." [24]

Possession of Supernatural Knowledge

Demons in the New Testament would speak through people to convey knowledge that otherwise could not have been known to the possessed individuals. Mentally ill people would not have ability to know facts that they have not acquired by normal means of learning. Koch states, "For example clairvoyance itself is never a sign of mental illness, and a mental patient will never be able to speak in a voice or a language he has previously not learned." [25]

Occult Phenomena

There is an aspect to demon activity that cannot be explained naturally.

If there are occurrences of poltergeists, levitations, trances, telepathy (and these can be ruled out as being optical illusions), then one is not dealing with ordinary mental illnesses.[26] These "most dramatic aspects" that were "frequently encountered" helped stump Isaac's panel of

---

[23] Kurt Koch and Alfred Lechler, *Occult Bondage and Deliverance*, 162-63.

[24] C. Fred Dickason, *Demon Possession and The Christian*, 228.

[25] Kurt Koch and Alfred Lechler, *Occult Bondage And Deliverance*, 58.

[26] See Henry and Mary Virkler, "Demonic Involvement in Human Life and Illness," *Journal of Psychology and Theology* 5(2) (1977), 100.

psychodiagnosticians at Berkeley.[27] He listed the following as indications of possession as opposed to mental illness: "some form of paranormal phenomena, such as poltergeist-type phenomena, telepathy, levitation or strength out of proportion to age; there is an impact on others; paranormal phenomena, stench, coldness or the feeling of an alien presence or that the patient has lost a human quality, is experienced by someone other than the patient." [28]

The Claim to be Possessed

Authors have already been quoted who assert that those who claim to be possessed are very likely not possessed. It is not unreasonable to think that demons operate with secrecy. Lechler writes, "While the mental patient will speak in extravagant tones of the demons he alleges to be living within, the possessed person avoids all mention of demons as long as no one approaches him on a spiritual level".[29]

The Effects of Therapy

If prayer and obedience to Scripture solves the problem, then it was not mental illness. If medicine solves the problem, it was not demon possession. In general this line of reasoning seems to be valid and commonly accepted. However, it does leave us with the situation where the person might exhibit abnormal behavior after both spiritual and medical help.

"Demons cannot be exorcised by phenothiazines, antidepressant drugs, or E.C.T." [30]

---

[27] T. Craig Isaacs, "*The Possessive State Disorder,*" 269.
[28] Ibid., 272.
[29] Kurt Koch and Alfred Lechler, *Occult Bondage and Deliverance,* 162.
[30] Walter Johnson, "Demon Possession and Mental Illness," *Journal of the American Scientific Affiliation* 34(3) (1982), 151.

"Hallucinations are cured by psychological treatment, while demon possession can be cured only by prayer and fasting as Christ indicated." [31]

"If a case of epilepsy can be cured medically, the demonic is not involved. If, however, the illness can be cured by prayer, then it was not an instance of epilepsy." [32]

"I have had hundreds of patients who came to see me because they thought they were demon-possessed. Scores of them heard "demon voices" telling them evil things to do.... I discovered that all of the 'demons' I was seeing were allergic to Thorazine and that, in nearly every case, a week or two on Thorazine made the 'demons' go away." [33]

When faced with the possible encounter of demon possession, a better assessment would result if both the New Testament symptoms of demon possession and the above suggestions for differentiating demon possession from mental illnesss would be kept in mind. One should consider whether mental illness can be ruled out, and then how many Biblical indicators of the demonic are present. In the final analysis, it is probable that real possession is so bizarre that one can think of no other explanation.

Dr. Van Gelder's account "A Case of Demon Possession" provides a situation where all present could think of no other explanation than demons. The situation was too unlike any mental illness or ordinary emotional problem. He relates a case of possession witnessed by a medical doctor (the boy's father),

---

31 Millard J. Sall, *Demon Possession or Psychopathology?*, 289.
32 Kurt Koch and Alfred Lechler, *Occult Bondage and Deliverance*, 10.
33 Danny Korem and Paul Meier, *The Fakers* (Grand Rapids: Baker, 1980), 160.

a psychologist, a pastor, a seminary professor, and several other well educated and rational observers. A number of phenomena he describes do overlap with the New Testament factors indicating possession.[34]

Dr. Van Gelder described a boy "springing to all fours snarling like an animal".[35] He said a crucifix flew onto the floor, and the nails in the wall melted.[36] The boy's face had the look of disdain, and his body writhed.[37] A third person's voice spoke through the boy in a "metallic" and "paralyzed" voice.[38] The episode ended with the boy praying to accept Christ as Savior. However, initially he cursed at all discussion of spiritual truth.[39]

In the situation described above, all present agreed on the diagnosis of demonic involvement just as all present agreed on the cases of possession in New Testament accounts. The supernatural aspects plus rational speech in a third person's voice with initial revulsion toward Christ ruled out ordinary mental illness.

What should a Christian worker do if he ever encounters a similar terrifying case where demon possession is the probable cause? Sometimes evangelical scholars who quarrel over details can really agree on essential points. That seems to be the case of strategies for dealing with demons among the authors consulted for this study.

---

[34] See Van Gelder, David W., "A Case of Demon Possession." *Journal of Pastoral Care* 41(2) (1987), 151-161.
[35] Ibid., 151.
[36] Ibid.
[37] Ibid., 153
[38] Ibid., 154.
[39] Ibid.

Controversial Strategies for Dealing with Demons

The writings of Mark I. Bubeck and C. Fred Dickason provoked a great discussion relative to issues involving demons.[40] The most extensive response was that of Alex Konya with criticism also coming from Tom Davis who wrote a review of Dickason's "Demon Possession and the Christian" for the *Grace Theological Journal.* [41]

There are many points of foundational agreement on what should be done if one thinks a ministry situation involves demonic influences. Nevertheless, a comparison of these and additional writings shows much friction over secondary points.

Confrontation

Dickason recommended a "confrontational test" in which a Christian worker challenges evil spirits to speak. He compared this to a psychological or medical test designed to reveal problems:

"There is a third means of investigating demonization, a confrontational test. After investigating symptoms and causes, the researcher may need to confirm the diagnosis with a command to the wicked spirits to manifest their presence within the client. With the client sufficiently prepared and with his consent, the researcher-counselor should ask that God control the situation completely and make clear to counselor

---

[40] Bubeck, Mark I. *Overcoming The Adversary.* Chicago: Moody, 1984; Bubeck, Mark I. *The Adversary.* Chicago: Moody, 1975; Dickason, C. Fred. *Demon Possession and the Christian* (Westchester IL: Crossway, 1987).

[41] Davis, Tom. "Review of Demon Possession and the Christian: A New Perspective by C. Fred Dickason." *Grace Theological Journal* 10 (Spring 1989), 89-94.

and client the presence of any demons that have invaded.... A string of challenging questions designed to determine difference in attitude of the counselee and the supposed invading demon may indeed disclose a genuine identification of a hostile demon." [42]

Critics responded to the "confrontational test" with confrontations and questions of their own.

"The classical orthodox position is to ask God for victory over Satan. Dickason wants to go a step further and speak directly with the demons." [43]

"Nowhere else in the New Testament can one find a single example of either Christ or anyone else using a test to determine demonization. The phenomenon of demonization was extreme and obvious." [44]

Some of the criticisms leveled against Dickason's confrontational test were weak. The Bible forbids speaking with evil spirits, but Dickason was clearly not recommending any sort of activity as a medium. He worked toward deliverance.

Konya pointed out the Bible alone is sufficient for ministry. [45] Davis also stressed "everything we need to know for life and godliness is presented in scripture".[46] This truth could imply a confrontational test is wrong because it goes

---

[42] C. Fred Dickason, *Demon Possession and the Christian*, 164. (See also pages 313 and 333.).

[43] Tom Davis, "Review of Demon Possession and the Christian", 94.

[44] Alex Konya, *Demons: A Biblically Based Perspective* 87, (see also p. 103).

[45] Ibid., 94-96.

[46] Davis, *Review of Demon Possession and the Christian*, 94.

beyond the Bible. However, those who suggest a confrontational test would no doubt agree with the sufficiency of Scripture. They might still suggest a confrontational test in order to diagnose the problem. Then one can better apply the Scriptures as a sufficient answer.

Dickason should not be described as a heretic for employing a confrontational test. Nevertheless, it may be questionable whether one needs to employ such a test if the traits of demon possession truly exist. In the New Testament possession was obvious to all.

Davis was correct in stating, "…demon possession was not secretive; but in every case recognized by all, including the unsaved. The Bible does not warn of secretive possession that can only be recognized and handled by a specialist. There is no mention of probing for the presence of demons." [47]

Evaluation of Possible Demonic Statements

Dickason quoted an interview with a demoniac in which a demon said demons can indwell and control believers.[48] How shall information that comes from those who seem to be possessed be evaluated? Complete skepticism is the best choice. Even if the words are those of a real demon, credence simply cannot be given to what can be learned from experiences with demons. It is probable that demons toyed with Jewish exorcists in Bible times. Demons would leave voluntarily in order to give the impression that the Jews had a valid ministry. However, such demons would later return to their victim (a possible understanding of Matt. 12:27, 43-45,

---

[47] Ibid., (see also John Warwick Montgomery ed., *Demon Possession*, 342 and Alex Konya, *Demons: A Biblically Based Perspective*, 31-32).
[48] C. Fred Dickason, *Demon Possession and the Christian*, 202-203.

and any attempts at exorcism by the "sons of Sceva" prior to Acts 19:13-17).[49] Konya warned, "since exorcism involves dealing with a foe that is cunning, deceiving, depraved, and unseen, misinterpreting experiences can be a real possibility."[50]

The Timing of Drug Therapy

When is the proper time to bring behavior changing drugs into the therapy? Should one try drugs as a first attempt or last resort?

These are not easy questions. Obviously, in a problem as complicated as demon possession it is wise for pastors and Christian physicians to cooperate.[51] There may be a general trend for physicians to want to employ drugs immediately in order to rule out medical problems whereas a pastor might feel that drugs should be used only after Biblical counseling fails. Dickason fears that the premature use of drugs could render a genuinely demon-possessed victim unable to resist wicked spirits.

"Now there are cases where chemical imbalance in the brain and physical and psychological illnesses may be helped by proper medical treatment. But demons do not leave when a person is so treated. The person may obtain some relief by development of better mental attitudes. But there are some depressant drugs that cause a state of passivity in which the demons find advantage. In such a state they are free to control,

---

[49] See Davis, *Review of Demon Possession and the Christian*, 93-94 and Alex Konya, *Demons: A Biblically Based Perspective*, 71,90,93.

[50] Ibid., 17.

[51] See Kurt Koch and Alfred Lechler, *Occult Bondage and Deliverance*, 13 and 37, and John Warwick Montgomery ed., *Demon Possession*, 307 and 359.

and the human is unable to resist them as he should. Treatment such as this does not help but adds to the confusion. Secular treatment of those actually demonized has resulted in their being constantly hospitalized and drugged, kept in a state of stupor, because the medical profession has not found an answer to their condition."[52]

One can sympathize with Dickason's reluctance to immediately embrace drug use as the initial therapy for behavioral trouble. Turning to medicine first for every emotional/behavioral problem stems from a world view in which man is regarded as an animal rather than a spiritual being. The causes of all his emotional problems are believed to arise from some medical problem. Sometimes behavioral problems are indeed rooted in physiological problems (for example, Alzheimer's or schizophrenia). Other times a spiritual/emotional problem generates a secondary medical problem (for example, drug addiction). However, many times a problem is purely a spiritual problem. While drugs may be part of the solution in those cases where spiritual problems have led to damage to our bodies, they can never be a full solution for those problems that are fundamentally or often totally spiritual in origin. They simply hide the real problems. Many are doing just that.

It is wise to refer counselees to a Christian physician when they have obvious physical problems, when they are unable to concentrate on Biblical counsel, and when they are suicidal. However, even in these cases medical therapies can only be part of the answer to spiritual problems. Even when drugs are necessary, they are not sufficient.

---

[52] C. Fred Dickason, *Demon Possession and The Christian*, 304-305.

Relative to possible demon possession, Biblical counsel should be attempted before medical help unless the one in need is in danger of immediate suicide or simply cannot think clearly enough to concentrate on counsel. Drugs can place people in a stupor. While a prescription may be needed as a partial help for spiritual problems that have led to secondary medical illnesses, medicine alone will not provide the full answer. There will be time enough for drug therapies if a person does not improve after hearing the gospel, prayers, and Scriptural teaching concerning Christ and the devil. In most cases only good can be expected to result from a brief delay to try spiritual help before use of drugs. In reality, unless it is an emergency situation, basic spiritual counseling could be completed before a person could ever make an appointment, see a physician, or obtain a prescription. Drugs may indeed be needed. The only issue here is the order in which they would be used and the degree of hope in them for a cure. If there is no deliverance by spiritual assistance, then the problem may be a purely medical one. Help with spiritual therapy for one who is believed to be possessed should at least be tried before turning to drugs as a means of restraint for the incurable. In situations where there is demonic involvement but continued rejection of Christ, would not suicide prevention and medical supervision still be in order after pastoral counseling has been ineffective or rejected?

Formal Liturgies and Rituals

The gospel accounts simply do not record any formal liturgies, magic words, procedures, or objects that could be used in ministry to those suffering from demons. Exorcism rituals are later additions by the church. The Lord used no set words, and He never touched a possessed person. [53]

"Probably the most striking feature of the exorcism performed by Jesus was the fact that they were without any accompaniment of the ritual incantation....in Neo-pentecostalism, the laying on of hands, ecstatic praying and singing, and other awe-inspiring rituals often accompany exorcisms. Again we note that this is a long way removed from the authoritative word of rebuke that came from Christ and his disciples." [54]

"The New Testament gives no records of gradual deliverance or protracted prayer meetings in connection with the ministries of either Jesus or the apostles....Proponents must admit that Jesus used no standard techniques..."[55]

Certainly man-made rituals can take extreme, even unbiblical, forms. However, should extreme abuse rule out all suggestions as to a formal plan for ministry to the demon possessed? Both Bubeck and Dickason offer suggested formal prayers for the demonized.[56] Others have suggested that missionaries could have better results in "heathen" lands by incorporating "exorcism rituals into their religious services."[57] John Warwick Montgomery agrees that the Bible does not give

---

[53] Basil Jackson, "Reflections on the Demonic: A Psychiatric Perspective," in *Demon Possession*, 264.
[54] Willem Berends, *The Biblical Criteria For Demon Possession*, 361 and 363.
[55] Alex Konya, *Demons: A Biblically Based Perspective*, 37.
[56] C. Fred Dickason, *Demon Possession and the Christian*, 255; Mark I. Bubeck, *Overcoming The Adversary* (Chicago: Moody, 1984), 26-27.
[57] Donald R. Jacobs, "Possession, Trance State, and Exorcism in Two East African Communities," in *Demon Possession*, 180. (See also page 336 for Luther and Wesley's views on exorcism rituals. Both urged prayers alone not "elaborate exorcist rites").

any rituals for exorcism but believes that it is not wrong to use them. He wonders if there is not just as much danger in the other extreme.

"But in our zeal to discard the unscriptural in the traditions of the church, we easily go to the other extreme, and fall uncritically to the mercy of individualistic, personalistic, experience-centered traditions of modern evangelical church life!" [58]

Perhaps there is a parallel in the use of man-made marriage vows. The Bible does not record any mandated vows, but there is nothing wrong in having them if they are administered in faith and honesty. Bubeck and Dickason offer their prayers as suggestions to help Christian leaders in dealing with a most difficult problem. They are not suggesting a liturgy but only sharing what they believe to be wise words of admittedly human origin. Finding great fault in this is being unnecessarily critical.

Clearer Strategies for Dealing with Demons

Despite disagreements on these secondary procedures, there are agreements on some more important issues. While evangelicals as a whole would argue over any "gift of exorcism", those in the non-charismatic school of thought unite on the point that the automatic ability to deliver from demons is a subset of healing. If the gift of healing ceased with the apostolic age, then we would no longer expect anyone to have powers to cast out demons. Cessationists disagree on the

---

[58] John Warwick Montgomery, "Exorcism: Is It for Real?" *Christianity Today* 18(21) (1974), 1185. Here Montgomery asserts Luther did permit exorcism wording as part of baptismal rites.

fine points of "deliverance ministry", but agree that ministers today cannot simply cast out demons at will.[59]

"Thus casting out demons in the Gospels could be regarded as a species of healings....In 2 Corinthians 12:12, Paul stated that miracles were distinguishing marks of apostleship....In the New Testament, no miracles ever occurred except at the hands of Jesus Himself or His apostles or those who were directly ministered to by an apostle." [60]

"There is no special gift of casting out demons. This was so in the first century of the church, and it is so now. Then it was part of the gift of miracles or possibly healing."[61]

To conclude that no one has a gift of healing/exorcism is not the same as ruling out all ministry by the church to the afflicted. Spiritual ministry to the sick does not cease because the gift of healing has ceased. Likewise, Christians must still minister to those who are demonized or those who have questions about demons because of their backgrounds in the occult or experiences with deliverance ministries. There is a

---

[59] Charismatics might not restrict their practice of what should be done with the demon-possessed to the conclusions in this study. However, much remains applicable. Whether one is charismatic or non-charismatic, there still is a need to consider the Biblical symptoms of demon possession closely before any conclusions or diagnoses. There also is a responsibility to screen for differences between mental illness and New Testament demon-possession. Finally, the suggested course of action proposed here does not contain anything that an evangelical charismatic should find objectionable.

[60] Alex Konya, *Demons: A Biblically Based Perspective*, 40 and 54. (see also pp. 74 and 80).

[61] C. Fred Dickason, *Demon Possession and The Christian*, 266. (see pp. 262-264, 330-331).

certain amount of irony in the fact that ministry to the demon-possessed goes back to the basics of Christian ministry on which all believers can agree. Despite the complexities and confusion of this topic, the best one could do to help the demon-possessed would be to follow simple ministry procedures that are common to most types of ministry. Are not these simple functions really the most important? Whether the result is deliverance, continued rejection of the truth, or no change, the following actions are morally and doctrinally true. They might yield help and could not possibly harm.

Prayers for the Afflicted

Christ taught His disciples the value of prayer in attempts to minister to the demonized. Whatever disagreements may surface on peripheral topics, all should agree on the need for complete dependence upon God in dealing with demons.

• "When He came into the house, His disciples began questioning Him privately, 'Why could we not drive it out?' And He said to them, 'This kind cannot come out by anything but prayer' " [Mark 9:28-29].

"...many so-called Biblical exorcisms may in fact be more correctly understood to be prayers for *divine* compulsion to remove these evil spirits from their victims. Many protracted prayer-battles fall into this category. These experiences, which are sometimes valid, are incorrectly called "Biblical exorcisms," when in fact they bear little resemblance to the demonic expulsions performed by Jesus and the apostles. We have no reason to believe that Jesus cannot sovereignly cast demons out even today, when earnest believers call upon Him to deliver the hapless victims of demonization. This is not,

however, a display of casting out demons as it was in the New
Testament. It is a different phenomenon." [62]

Prayer ought to be an obvious part of any ministry to those
suffering from demons. However, it is not that some magical
words mumbled in a prayer give immediate relief. The faith
expressed by prayer and the object of the prayer, God the
Father, Son, and Holy Spirit, are the real hopes for any
deliverance.

Faith in God's Power

Only a prayer that expresses faith could be of benefit in
deliverance from demons. Faith in a situation involving
demons means Christ's servant fully trusts that Christ has
power over darkness. Perhaps the victim himself may not
initially request deliverance from Satan, but if there is to be
any deliverance, it would only come about by the Person and
power of the Lord Jesus Christ, not a special "gift" or "power"
inherent in an "exorcist". Christ taught the value of faith for
those who desire others to be delivered from demons.

• "And a Canaanite woman from that region came out and
began to cry out, saying, 'Have mercy on me, Lord, Son of
David; my daughter is cruelly demon-possessed,'....Then Jesus
said to her, 'O woman, your faith is great; it shall be done for
you as you wish.' And her daughter was healed at once" [Matt.
15:22,28].

• "And He answered them and said, 'O unbelieving
generation, how long shall I be with you? How long shall I put

---

[62] Alex Konya, *Demons: A Biblically Based Perspective*, 92. See also C.
Fred Dickason, *Demon Possession and the Christian*, 47.

up with you? Bring him to Me!' They brought the boy to Him. When he saw Him, immediately the spirit threw him into a convulsion, and falling to the ground, he began rolling around and foaming at the mouth. And He asked his father, 'How long has this been happening to him?' And he said, 'From childhood. It has often thrown him both into the fire and into the water to destroy him. But if You can do anything, take pity on us and help us!' And Jesus said to him, " 'If You can'? All things are possible to him who believes." Immediately the boy's father cried out and said, 'I do believe; help my unbelief' " [Mark 9:19-24].

The incident involving Jewish exorcists in the book of Acts shows that a mere magical use of Christ's name will not help the possessed. There must be a genuine faith in His power before there can be real deliverance.

• "But also some of the Jewish exorcists, who went from place to place, attempted to name over those who had the evil spirits the name of the Lord Jesus, saying, 'I adjure you by Jesus who Paul preaches'. Seven sons of one Sceva, a Jewish chief priest, were doing this. And the evil spirit answered and said to them, 'I recognize Jesus, and I know about Paul, but who are you?' And the man, in whom was the evil spirit, leaped on them and subdued all of them and overpowered them, so that they fled out of that house naked and wounded" [Acts 19:13-16].

While prayers made in faith in Christ's name form a possible basis for deliverance, no doubt a victim's will plays an even more important role in the matter. The message of the cross is the real key to breaking demonic powers. Those influenced by demons must trust in the Lord Jesus Christ as Savior to have power over Satan.

The Gospel

Regardless of the debate over whether believers can be demon possessed, it is a fair conclusion that believers cannot be involuntarily possessed by demons (see references below concerning Christ's power over Satan). Therefore, if a person becomes a believer and wishes no further involvement with demons, they must depart. How could anyone object to a strong gospel presentation in situations involving probable demon possession? Even if there might be deliverance without salvation as a response to prayers for a victim, it would not be a true or lasting victory (see Matthew 12:43-45). The gospel is the power of God unto salvation (Romans 1:16). Despite all their debates, the experts in this area seem to agree on this point.

"If there is doubt that the person is a genuine Christian, he must hear, understand, and accept the gospel."[63]

"And any person who accepts Jesus as his Lord and Savior, and who makes it his aim to follow Him, will be able to find deliverance from all forms of demoniac oppression." [64]

"There can be no exorcism when the True Exorcist is rejected in favor of a 'gross' product, when swine are preferred to the Savior. Perhaps demon influence and possession are increasing because men choose to possess their demons." [65]

"For the unbeliever, Christ must be put on positionally, this means turning to Christ as his personal Savior. This is the only

---

[63] C. Fred Dickason, *Demon Possession and The Christian*, 336.
[64] Kurt Koch and Alfred Lechler, *Occult Bondage and Deliverance*, 192.
[65] D. G. Kehl, "Diabolism in Modern Literature," in *Demon Possession*, 134.

true and ultimate solution for his problems with demons. Apart from putting on Christ, the unbeliever remains in Satan's realm and has no ultimate defense against renewed demonic attack, even if demons have been previously cast out." [66]

Scriptures Asserting Christ's Power over Satan

John Warwick Montgomery asserts, "Whatever the forms employed in exorcism, everything must focus upon the power and strength of Christ".[67] There are many useful texts when helping one thought to be possessed or one wishing to convert from the occult to Christ. All these passages stress Christ's power over Satan: John 8:32-36, 12:31, 16:11, 17:15; Romans 6:14,17-18, 20, 8:38-39; Eph. 5:8; Col. 1:13, 2:15; Heb. 2:14-15; James 4:7; 1 Peter 5:8-9; 1 John 3:8, 4:4, 5:18.

Disposal of Occultic/Idolatrous Objects

Acts chapter 19 gives a Scriptural basis for demanding the destruction of occultic objects. Therefore, it is proper to insist that anyone suspected of being demon-possessed part with any object that could have occultic connections.

- Many also of those who had believed kept coming, confessing and disclosing their practices. And many of those who practiced magic brought their books together and began burning them in the sight of everyone; and they counted up the price of them and found it fifty thousand pieces of silver" [Acts 19:18-19].

- "Little children, guard yourselves from idols" [1 John 5:21].

---

[66] Alex Konya, *Demons: A Biblically Based Perspective,* 114.
[67] John Warwick Montgomery, *"Exorcism: Is it for Real?"*, 1186.

Severance of Occultic Associations

Many new Christians find that they must break off ties to their unsaved friends in order to avoid a negative influence. This would be even more necessary for those who have been saved from demon possession and/or involvement in the occult.

* "No, but I say that the things which the Gentiles sacrifice, they sacrifice to demons, and not to God: and I do not want you to become sharers in demons. You cannot drink the cup of the Lord and the cup of demons; you cannot partake of the table of the Lord and the table of demons" [1 Corinthians 10:20-21].

* "... what harmony has Christ with Belial..." [2 Cor. 6:15].

Conclusion

In an ideal world servants of Christ would never encounter Satan-worshipers or those suspected of being demon possessed. However, in a fallen world "the god of this world" (2 Cor. 4:4) has his adherents. Caution must be exercised in any diagnosis of demon possession for great harm can be done to a person's emotions through a well meaning but ignorant and/or hasty misdiagnosis. The safest course is a strict insistence upon the presence of the Biblical symptoms of demon possession with a knowledge of some basic differences between demon possession and mental illness. Perhaps as in Bible times true cases of possession are so terrifying and overwhelming that a spiritual and Biblically informed Christian will know when he deals with the real thing.

There is debate over incidental features of this kind of ministry, but who can object to the basic forms of ministry that should be common to dealing with all unsaved people? They are all, possessed or not, trapped in Satan's domain and are his children (see John 8:44; 1 John 5:19). Perhaps the greatest lesson learned from this topic is that simple types of ministry are the most important types of ministry approved by believers of all denominations and theological systems. Demon possession is an extremely complex subject, but ministry involves the basics: prayer, faith in God's power, the message of salvation by faith in Christ, Bible texts asserting Christ's power over Satan, and severance from occultic objects and associations.

"Since then the children share in flesh and blood, He Himself likewise also partook of the same, so that through death He might render powerless him who had the power of death, that is, the devil, and might free those who through fear of death were subject to slavery all their lives" [Heb. 2:14-15].

BIBLIOGRAPHY

General Works

Bubeck, Mark I. *Overcoming The Adversary* (Chicago: Moody, 1984).

Bubeck, Mark I. *The Adversary* (Chicago: Moody, 1975).

Collins, Gary R. *Can You Trust Psychology?* (Downer's Grove: IVP, 1988).

De Haan, Richard W. *Satan, Satanism, and Witchcraft* (Grand Rapids: Zondervan, 1972).

Demon Experiences in Many Lands: Strange Occurrences in Mission Fields of the World, A Compilation (Chicago: Moody, 1960).

Dickason, C. Fred. *Angels: Elect and Evil* (Chicago: Moody, 1975).

Dickason, C. Fred. *Demon Possession and the Christian* (Westchester: Crossway Books, 1987).

Ensign, Grayson H. and Edward Howe. *Bothered? Bewildered? Bewitched? Your Guide To Practical Spiritual Healing* (Cincinnati: Recovery, 1984).

Gumprecht, Jane. *New Age Health Care: Holy or Holistic?* (Orange: Promise Publishing, 1988).

Koch, Kurt. *Demonology Past and Present,* rep. ed. (Grand Rapids: Kregel, 1973).

Koch, Kurt E., and Alfred Lechler. *Occult Bondage and Deliverance,* rev. ed. (Grand Rapids: Kregel, 1973).

Konya, Alex. *Demons: A Biblically Based Perspective* (Schaumburg: Regular Baptist, 1990).

Korem, Danny, and Paul Meier. *The Fakers* (Grand Rapids: Baker, 1980).

Lindsey, Hal. *Satan Is Alive and Well on Planet Earth* (Grand Rapids: Zondervan, 1972).

McDowell, Josh and Dan Stewart. *Understanding the Occult* (San Bernadino: Here's Life, 1982).

Martin, Walter. *The New Age Cult* (Minneapolis: Bethany House, 1989).

Montgomery, John Warwick, ed. *Demon Possession* (Minneapolis: Bethany House, 1976).

Montgomery, John Warwick. *Principalities and Powers.* rev. ed. (Minneapolis: Dimension Books, 1975).

Nelson, Marion. *Why Christians Crack Up* (Chicago: Moody, 1960).

Nevius, John L. *Demon Possession,* rev. ed. (Grand Rapids: Kregel, 1968).

Peck, M. Scott. *People of the Lie: The Hope For Healing Human Evil* (New York: Simon and Schuster, 1983).

Penn-Lewis, Jessie. *War on the Saints,* rev. ed. (Fort Washington: Literature Crusade, 1977).

Pentecost, I. Dwight. *Your Adversary The Devil* (Grand Rapids: Zondervan, 1969).

Schwarz, Ted, and Duane Empey. *Satanism* (Grand Rapids: Zondervan, 1988).

Unger. Merrill F. *Demons in the World Today* (Wheaton: Tyndale, 1971).

Waterhouse, Steven W. "Demonology", "Satanology", *Not By Bread Alone* (Amarillo: Westcliff, 2000).

Wiersbe, Warren W. *The Strategy of Satan* (Wheaton: Tyndale, 1979).

Wilson, Clifford, and John Weldon. *Occult Shock and Physic Forces* (San Diego: Master Books, 1980).

PERIODICALS

Bach, Paul S. "Demon Possession and Psychopathology: A Theological Relationship." *Journal of Psychology and Theology* 7(1) (1979):22-30.

Berends, Willem. "The Biblical Criteria For Demon Possession." *Westminster Theological Journal* 37(3) (1975): 342-365.

Davis, Tom. "Review of Demon Possession and the Christian: A New Perspective by C. Fred Dickason." *Grace Theological Journal* 10 (Spring 1989): 89-94.

Fuller, J. Williams. "A Psychological Profile of Biblical Demons: The Fear of Death." *Journal of the American Scientific Affiliation* 35(2) (1983): 84-87.

Hexham, Irving. "Theology Exorcism and Amplification of Deviancy." *Evangelical Quarterly* 49(2) (1977): 111-116.

Isaacs, T. Craig. "The Possessive States Disorder. The Diagnosis of Demonic Possession." *Pastoral Psychology* 34(4) (1986): 264-287.

Johnson. Walter. "Demon Possession and Mental Illness." *Journal of the American Scientific Affiliation* 34(3) (1982): 149-154.

Koteskey, Ronald L. "Abandoning the Psyche to Secular Treatment." *Christianity Today* 23(18) (1979): 985-987.

Koteskey, Ronald L. "Toward The Development of a Christian Psychology: Adjustment and Maladjustment." *Journal of Psychology and Theology* 7(3) (1979): 176-186.

Montgomery. John Warwick. "Exorcism: Is It For Real?" *Christianity Today* 18-213 (1974): 1183-1186.

"Occult: A Substitute Faith." *Time* 19 June 1972, pp.62-68.

Otis. Gerald E. "Power Encounter: The Way to Muslim Breakthrough." *Evangelical Missions Quarterly* 16(4) (1980): 217-220.

Sall, Millard J. "A Response To Demon Possession and Psychopathology: A Theological Relationship." *Journal of Psychology and Theology* 7(1) (1979): 27-30.

Sall, Millard J. "Demon Possession or Psychopathology?: A Critical Differentiation". *Journal of Psychology and Theology 4(4)(1976):*286-290.

Southard, Samuel. *"Demonizing and Mental Illness: The Problem of Assessment."*Pastoral Psychology 34(4) (1986): 264-287.

Van Gelder, David W. "A Case of Demon Possession." *Journal of Pastoral Care* 41(2) (1987): 151-161.

Virkler, Henry A., and Mary B. "Demonic Involvement in Human Life and Illness." *Journal of Psychology and Theology* 5(2) (1977): 95-102.

Zuck, Roy B., "The Practice of Witchcraft in the Scriptures." *Bibliotheca Sacra* 128 (October-December 1971,): 351-60.

THE SANCTITY
OF
LIFE

A Sermon on the Right-to-Life

Abortion is *wrong* whether viewed
theologically, philosophically, scientifically,
or medically... God is interested in the
development of the unborn from their
very beginning..."So often in the abortion
argument the mother says, 'I can do
whatever I want with this baby, I own it'.
No you don't. God owns the children..."

A study of the Bible texts mentioning the
unborn based upon the original
Hebrew and Greek languages

This material on tape and in booklet form has been given to all members of
the United States Senate and the U.S. House of Representatives twice. It was
used by Care Net to train crisis pregnancy center staff and to motivate
churches to action.

THE SANCTITY OF LIFE
(Young and Old)

A Sermon on Abortion and Euthanasia

On Monday, they sang, Holy, Holy, Holy.

Following a past presidential inauguration, the nation watched the entire federal government go to the National Cathedral on Monday and sing "Holy, Holy, Holy". It is the same song we sing. They used the same great evangelical Christian words that we sing blessing the Trinity. The Executive, Judicial, House, and Senate all sang praise to God on Monday. Then the rest of that week many of the same officials spoke against the Sanctity of Life as they opposed the annual march that laments the tragic Roe vs. Wade decision. We do, from time to time, give the Biblical reasons for the preservation of life. It worries me that we have a whole generation that has grown up under a system where abortion is legal and where euthanasia may someday be legal. We now have adults born after 1973. They may not know the Biblical reasons why evangelicals oppose abortion. I want to start out by giving them to you. For many of you, this will be a review. For some of you, it may be the first time you have heard the case for the right to life using the Bible.

THE BIBLICAL VIEW

The first thing we're going to see is God is *interested and involved* in the development of the unborn from their very beginning. Please turn in your Bibles to two passages that support that fact, Job Chapter 10 and Psalm 139. Psalm 139:13-16 is the more important passage, but to be inclusive, we will also read a text dealing with the unborn which comes from Job 10, beginning at verse eight. We'll begin with the Job passage and spend more time in the Psalm 139 passage. I will begin reading in Job 10, verse eight, *"thy hands fashioned and made me altogether, and wouldst thou destroy me?"*

Thy Hands Fashioned me.

Job is talking about his sickness. He says, *"Remember now that thou hast made me as clay; would you turn me into dust again? Did you not pour me out like milk and curdle me like cheese, clothe me with skin and flesh, knit me together with bones and sinews? Thou hast granted me life and loving kindness; and thy care has preserved my spirit."* The Hebrew word for "fashioned" in this verse is used many times in the Hebrew Bible as the word "pain." It is really odd. Fashioned equals pain. Why? Have you ever heard the phrase someone took "great pains" to do something? It means they were very intimately involved in it. They worked very, very hard at something. They were intensely interested in it. It was a top priority. That is why the Hebrew word for pain goes along with the Hebrew word for fashioned here. It means very intense involvement. When we take great pains to do something correctly, it is something we care about. Job is saying when I was unborn, when I was being developed, when the bones and sinews and skin and the organs, when it was all coming together, God took great pains in my development. That ought to prove the first point of our thesis: God is intimately involved in the development of the unborn.

God Is Involved.

We also see this truth in Psalm 139, beginning at verse 13. I am going to read this text and give a lesson on the significant Hebrew words contained in it, Psalm 139 beginning in verse 13. We are going to have different translations in all of these texts.

Again, I have read all of the Hebrew words, and we will be studying from the original Hebrew. Verse 13, *"For thou didst form my inward parts,* (the margin might say kidneys), *Thou didst weave me in my mother's womb. I will give thanks to thee, for I am fearfully and wonderfully made. Wonderful are thy works, and my soul knows it very well. My frame was not hidden from Thee when I was made in secret, and skillfully wrought in the depths of the earth."* That is poetry; it just means a secret place no one can see. Verse 16: *"Thine eyes have seen my unformed substance."*

Then the writer talks about the life span that God would have willed: *"and in thy book they were all written, the days that were ordained for me, when as yet, there was not one of them."* Verse 13 says: *Thou didst form my inward parts."* If you are reading out of the King James Version, it will say, *"Thou hast possessed my (inward parts)."* This is the correct translation of the Hebrew text. The Hebrew word is *kah-nah*. If you follow this word in the eighty-four times it is used in the Old Testament, you will find very often it means to acquire, to buy something, to own something. It is used of Ruth, in the book of Ruth, when relatives were going to redeem or purchase a field. Why do I push this? I push it because actually what he is saying is, "God, you **possessed** me, and you **owned** me when I was unborn. You fashioned me, but more than that you **owned** me."

God Owns the Unborn.

So often in the abortion argument, the mother says, "I can do whatever I want with this baby, I own it." **No, you don't.** *God owns the children.* The unborn belong to Him. That is why I am going back and insisting in this particular case that the King James translation is correct. The Hebrew word means you **owned** me. Unless you leave it as it stands, with the word "possess" or "own", you miss the application. God **owns** the unborn.

The text also says, *"He formed their inward parts."* The Hebrew word for "inward parts" is kidneys. You may have that in your margin. There are twelve times in the Hebrew Old Testament that the word kidney is used of humans. It never means the physical organ when it is used of humans. It does not mean the physical organ that cleanses blood that we generally associate with the kidneys. The Old Testament authors are thinking of kidney here in the same way we use the word "heart." They are thinking of the place where the innermost person resides, the place of thinking, the place of emotions, and the place of the soul. I do not know what the translators do with that. If they translate literally, and say kidney, we are never going to catch the meaning. To a Hebrew, a kidney was what the heart would be to a modern mindset. You are talking about a soul. You are talking about the non-material part of man. Verse 13 is saying God, you owned me, and you developed my soul when I was within my mother. You will see the immediate significance of that point. Some part, at least, of man's non-material nature or some part of the soul is present from the beginning. Some part of that which was created in the image of God and is holy is present from the very beginning, and God owns it.

The Unborn are God's Work.

Now, in verse 14, there is one phrase I would like to pick out. It is the third phrase: *"Wonderful are Thy works."* The unborn child is a work of God. He claims every child. So, when we destroy that work of God or oppose that work, we are opposing what He wants to do. We are opposing God. All these truths should establish the main point. **God is interested and involved in the development of the unborn.** They have spiritual natures and He owns them; it is His work and His business, and those that oppose that work are opposing God.

Now we will look at the second point in the argument, and

it is that **God sees the unborn as individuals.** He sees their whole future ahead of them. He does not look at them as we would. He sees their whole human potential. A couple of texts that would show this would be Jeremiah 1 and Psalm 51. Please find those chapters. While you are turning there, I will convey my feelings to you.

There is cleansing and forgiveness.

Whenever I talk about a topic like this, I am concerned there probably are ladies here who have had abortions. That may surprise you, but it does not surprise me a bit. It is hard to talk about a topic that conveys the fact that abortion is a great wickedness, and yet in the same message, convey God's grace. So, I do not want to leave that out. I do want you to know there is cleansing, and there is forgiveness. First, faith in the cross settles our relationship before God. **Trusting what Christ has done on the cross makes us clean and whole again.** I do not want you to lose that.

The goal of today's message is to show that abortion is a great evil. So, it will not all be gracious in tone, but do not leave out the truth that there is cleansing, and there is forgiveness for all who trust in the Lord Jesus Christ. We are looking at how God knows the unborn as individuals with a complete destiny.

God knew me before I was born.

Jeremiah 1:5 is a wonderful passage to see that fact. We will read that one next. *Before I formed you in the womb, I knew you.* Obviously, God is involved again. He knew the unborn Jeremiah as an individual, which is our second point. He sees unborn children as individuals with a separate identity and an entire destiny. *"Before I formed you in the womb, I knew you. Before you were born, I consecrated you: I have appointed you a* _prophet to the nations._" When Jeremiah was not yet born, God could view him and look at his whole life span. Understand that God knows the entire future. He knows the entire lost potential if the future should be cut off. He looked at the unborn and knew his name would be Jeremiah. He looked at the unborn Jeremiah and knew he would deliver His message. He knew everything that would ever happen to him. When God looks at an unborn baby today, He sees the same thing. He does not just see tissue, bones, cartilage, and organs. He does not see, as some do, just the physical remains of an infant being aborted. God knows what name that child would have had. Would it have been Mary or Charles? He knows the entire life span: what skills the child would have developed, what difficulties the child would have had, where there would have been successes, where there would have been failures. He knows the infant's whole future. So while some people can put on blinders and rationalize that this unborn baby can go out in the trash with the medical wastes, God does not look at the child as just tissue. God sees the entire human potential and knows everything about each person before he or she was ever born. As Christians God's view should be our view. The unborn baby has life and has a whole potential ahead of him. He or she has great value.

The soul from conception

The passage in Psalm 51:5 will also look at the individual identity of each unborn baby and say something about the soul, the immaterial being. Psalm 51:5: _"Behold, I was brought forth in iniquity, and in sin my mother conceived me."_ At first you would not think this contributes much to the argument for the right to life, but what David is saying is that from the very beginning of conception he had a sin nature. Now, I do not know for certain whether the soul was present in full form from the very beginning or that in a mysterious, unknown way, each soul grows and develops. I do think souls are passed on from parents to children.

It could be that they develop right along with the body. That is for another sermon. It is called Traducianism, but we cannot go into that now.

Abortion is evil. It may be murder.

To say that from conception there is part of the sin nature present means that part of the soul has to be present from conception. The sin nature is not a biological part, is not an appendage, nor is it an organ. The sin nature is part of a person's soul. To say that the sin nature begins at conception is to say that the soul, at least in germ form, has to begin at conception. To destroy the unborn child destroys part or all of a human soul. While I would accept a range of conclusions here, the very least you can say is abortion is a great wickedness; or you could conclude that it is murder. At the very least, you are destroying some element of a human soul. This is because the sin nature is present from conception. That is what David is saying in Psalm 51. We are all conceived in sin.

Another verse that helps is Luke 1:44. Luke 1:44 is the Christmas passage where John the Baptist is inside of his mother, Elizabeth, and Mary comes to visit her cousin. The unborn John the Baptist leaps for joy in his mother's womb. What is joy if it is not an emotion? What is an emotion if it is not a part of the human soul? John the Baptist, somehow, was an unborn child experiencing the joy of emotion being in the presence of the unborn Messiah. Theologians look at this and say here is a display of emotion in the unborn. This, too, is part of a person's soul.

Point number one: **God is interested and involved in the development of the unborn.** Point number two: **He views them as individuals with a complete destiny (having souls).**

According to the Law of Moses

Now, we are going to look at a passage in Exodus to see that **God considers abortion a great iniquity.** I am going to read it from the New International Version, but if you would like to turn to Exodus 21; I will pause a second for you to find that chapter. The translators do not all agree on the translation. Rather than give you all the technicalities, I hope you will just trust me on this one. I have spent many, many hours studying this in Hebrew and the New International Version is the correct translation here. What it is going to say is that an accidental abortion, according to the Law of Moses, required the death penalty. It says even an accidental abortion was deemed to be a very severe iniquity under the Law of Moses. This is Exodus 21 beginning at verse 22: *"If men, who are fighting, hit a pregnant woman and she gives birth prematurely; but there is no serious injury, the offender must be fined whatever the husband demands and the court allows."* I will stop right there. In this first situation, two men are involved in a fight and a pregnant woman tries to intervene, apparently to protect her husband. If she is injured to the point of going into labor, but she survives and the baby survives, the Law of Moses required a financial penalty. The husband wants to be compensated, and if the court agrees, there is a financial fine.

Mother and child equal in value

The next phrase continues, *"But if there is serious injury, you are to take life for life."* Then it goes on, *"eye for an eye, tooth for tooth, hand for hand, foot for foot"*, etc. That is a common phrase: *"eye for eye, tooth for tooth."* If there is serious injury, if either the mother or the unborn baby dies in the scuffle, they are to execute, as capital punishment, the person who caused the miscarriage. Trust me on this one. This is the correct translation. This is a very key passage because other translations translate it differently with different conclusions. The NIV is right.

Under the Law of Moses, even if there were an accidental abortion, it was considered a great iniquity, and you were to inflict capital punishment because of the death of that baby. A second conclusion here is that the baby is equal in value to the mother.

How does God see deliberate abortion?

Reason with me on this. If an accidental abortion would be grounds for capital punishment under the Law of Moses, how do you think God views an abortion performed on purpose? If an accidental abortion was a capital offense (because the baby's life was equal to the mother) **the Law of Moses clearly would have imposed a death penalty for deliberate abortion**. Exodus 21 is not an accidental miscarriage or a natural one. This is a fight, a lady is injured. It would be like a car wreck today. Consider a case where the driver was under the influence, and the unborn baby died accidentally. The Law of Moses would demand capital punishment. This is far more severe than we would do today. What must God think of the deliberate destruction of the unborn?

God is patient, but He has limits.

I do not know why God puts up with America. We deserve judgment. Chastisement would probably be good for us. He is very patient with us. He has to be filled with wrath over the destruction of a million and a half children a year, and these are not accidents. Have you ever thought about how many a million and a half individuals are? I will give you a weird illustration. A million and a half are about how many cars the Ford Motor Company produces a year. Do you see many Fords while you are driving around? They are everywhere, are they not? So are abortions. They are just hidden. Yet they are everywhere. Now, the Biblical evidence alone is sufficient for me to settle the argument over abortion.

We have used the Bible first because it is the primary authority. For those who respect the Bible, that ought to be the end of the debate. It is enough for me. I know the answer on this one. I know what to teach my children, and I know how to pray for the way they will live. The matter of abortion is already settled. This tells me that in addition to whatever else God wants me to do, He would want me to care about Crisis Pregnancy Centers. He would want me to teach my children and the youth of our church and anybody I can reach about the value of life. He wants me to pray and give toward that end. The Bible alone is the final authority for me.

Now, I would like to add medical, legal, and philosophical arguments, because when we discuss this topic with people, many of them have no interest in what the Bible says about abortion or any other subject.

THE MEDICAL VIEW

It is a child, not a raccoon.

Let us look first at a little medicine or a little biology. From the moment of conception is the child living or dead? It is living. It is going to grow. Is it a carrot? Is it a raccoon? Is it a daisy? No. The child has 46 chromosomes. It is not going to be a carrot, a raccoon, or a daisy. **It is alive, by the definition of life, and it is not any of these other things.** If you want to know the truth, the developing child is different from the mother. The child is part father and part mother, so it is distinct. It is alive, it has 46 chromosomes, it is not raccoon, daisy, blueberry, or anything other than human, and it is distinct from the mother. I am not a geneticist, but I am told that if you could take a gene map of the mother's genes, and a gene map of the beginning life and just look at the maps, just the structure, and ask experts which one is the mother and which one is the new conception, they cannot tell the difference. Both have all the human information. Obviously, if you look at the individuals, you can tell a difference between mother and unborn child. But if you look at the map of the information, if you look at the map of the gene codes, you cannot tell a difference. You would have to look at pictures of the unborn baby and pictures of the mother to tell which is which because both have equal genetic information for humanity. The child is *alive*. It is not dead. It is not a carrot; it has 46 chromosomes.

The child is living!

Let us look at this from a little different angle. I loved going to the seminary in Washington, D.C. because I was able to observe the congressional committee hearings, listen to the debates, and go down and watch the Congress. I went to hearings on abortion. Senator East from North Carolina was presiding. He was disabled and could not walk. He was questioning a medical professor from Harvard, and he was really mad. "You mean you can go to the moon and you can go to the bottom of the ocean and you cannot tell me whether something is alive or dead?" What else is a developing child but alive? Take the common medical definitions for death and reverse them. Choose whichever definition for death you want. Take the definition and reverse it. If we say the absence of a heartbeat is death, then life begins at 18 days, and abortion causes death. If we say the absence of a brain wave is death, life begins at 43 days. *Nearly all abortions take place after that.* The statistics I have indicate that all abortions do. I am no expert, so I do not know whether I can say *all,* but the chart I have says all abortions take place after 43 days. So, if the definition of death would be the absence of the brain wave, or the cessation of the heartbeat, then abortion causes death. Take definitions of death and reverse them, and the unborn have life whether it is the heartbeat or brain wave. Whether looking at it genetically or looking at it medically, the developing children are alive. They are not going to be carrots. Children are *humans.*

Abortion stops the heartbeat. Abortion stops the brainwave. Abortion causes pain. What else is abortion but the destruction of life?

THE PHILOSOPHICAL VIEW

Let me apply some logic. Philosophy. The first argument was medical, this one is philosophical. I remember one congressional committee meeting in Washington where there were people with signs reading, "AAA." I wondered what they were doing there. Travelers? Cars? No, they were "Atheists Against Abortion." I did not know what this organization was. They were in the committee meeting with big signs. They were able to reason from logic alone that abortion is evil.

To examine a philosophical idea, it should be taken to its logical outcome. When we do this, abortion is irrational. Every argument for abortion is the same argument for death for those that are already born. Therefore, there is something wrong with pro-abortion logic. Every argument for abortion is an equal argument for killing those already born. Let me show you.

By this logic, those who are poor should not live.

The abortionist says, "well, these are going to be born into poverty. They ought not to live. Poverty is terrible." However, would this not be the same argument for killing the majority in Africa, South America, and Asia? Again, we are told they are poor. If poor people should not live, then why not rid ourselves of all poor people. Every argument for abortion is an equal argument for murder, for infanticide, and for even killing adults. So something is wrong with such reasoning. Look how much poverty there is all over the world. Abortion logic could be the same argument for killing those already born.

Another assertion is that the unborn might not have high intelligence. First of all, who defines intelligence? This really worries me about how some define intelligence. I have read liberal material that compares religious believers to wild animals that may have to be caged. The same material argues that parents should be prevented from informing their children about the flaws of evolution. Apparently, I am ignorant because I am a conservative. Who is going to define intelligence anyway? We say this unborn baby may not be intelligent. That is an equal argument for killing all kinds of people pro-abortionists do not think possess intelligence. Something is wrong with such logic. Take it to its conclusion. It ends in irrationality. **Every argument for abortion is an argument for death of people that are already born**, from infants to old people.

Ten ounces and alive!

What about logic and the concept of viability? Viability is where the child is able to live on its own. The child is far enough along in its development that it could live on its own and would not need to be within the mother for any more nurture and development. The period of viability keeps getting shorter and shorter. Doctors keep saving smaller and smaller babies. I saved an article about a baby which doctors saved weighing only ten ounces at birth. I don't know if the record has been lowered since then or not. *They saved a baby that weighed ten ounces!* Fifteen years later a newspaper article revealed that the child was progressing well in high school, excelling in music. How much smaller viability can go I do not know, but it is very poor logic to say that babies need not have the right-to-life unless there is viability. Viability keeps getting shorter and shorter and shorter. By such logic, human life keeps being redefined. Also, you have this madness (talk about twisted logic) where **babies who are smaller, and more immature, weighing less than a pound are being saved in one end of the hospital, and babies weighing**

several times more are being aborted at the other end of the hospital. I am not using the Bible here. I am just talking about simple logic. *This is madness!* They are saving the little preemies who are smaller and aborting the infants more developed!

I have pictures in my office. You ought to see them. You ought to see an aborted child at nineteen weeks. I will let you look right into their eyes. This is a saline solution so they are not all carved up. *This is a child.* No one could argue with it. If any of you would like to see an aborted child, I have pictures in my office. So, how logical are the reasonings of pro-abortion advocates? When you are saving children who are smaller than the ones you are killing, what sense is that?

THE LEGAL VIEW

So far, we have considered the Bible, which, to you and me, is the most important authority. We have talked about medicine and logic. Next I would like to talk about law.

Once I went to a lecture at the Supreme Court. Harry Blackmun came out in his robes, and the clerk of the court cried, "all rise." Everyone stood up. I was in the front row. I was sitting very close to Harry Blackmun. He wrote the Roe vs. Wade decision. C. Everett Koop, former Surgeon General, has summarized Blackmun's view this way: "We need not resolve the question of when life begins."[1] *Why not?* Because a court says so? We need not decide when life begins? We do not have to think about it? If one feels the unborn cannot absolutely be proven to be human, then it is acceptable to destroy them? Okay, for the sake of

---

[1] C. Everett Koop, *The Right to Live; The Right to Die* (Wheaton IL: Tyndale House, 1976), page 39.

of argument, let me agree for a few minutes. Let us just say we do not know whether the unborn are living or dead. I do not agree with that, but let us go along with such reasonings. We do not know for certain whether they are human, so we can legally destroy them. I would like to evaluate that statement for its logic. They might be alive or they might be dead. They might be human, they might not be human. We do not know, and we do not have to think about it. We do not have to think about whether the child is alive or dead.

Let us apply that to other areas of life. Let us say I am hunting. I am deer hunting. I see movement over there in the woods. Am I not responsible for knowing whether it is human before I shoot? And if it even *might* be human, do you not think I ought to give the benefit of the doubt and refrain from shooting? Even if I do not know for certain, even if there is a *slight possibility* (and they will all concede it is a possibility that the unborn are human), I should not shoot. Even if it is only *possible* that a human is over there in the woods, then I better not kill it. **I should give the benefit of the doubt to the preservation of life simply because the target *might* be human.** There were a couple teachers in my high school. They were deer hunting, and one of them killed the other. One saw movement in the bushes, and he was not sure if it was human or not, but it was moving so he shot. He killed the other teacher. You and I would be responsible for knowing for certain that a target for death is positively not human. It is not enough to say, "well, I do not know whether it is or not, I will kill it anyway." Suppose that an ambulance comes up to an accident scene and the EMT asks the question, "Are the people in this car alive or dead?" "We do not know", the bystanders say. Based on that reply, should the ambulance leave without knowing with certainty the condition of the injured? The very possibility that they may be alive means we must protect and help them. The false argument easily goes from "maybe they are alive, maybe they are not" to "we do not know

and we do not care." If the unborn *might* be human, then we have
to take action on the side of life.

Whether you look at abortion through the Bible, medicine,
philosophy or law, abortion is crazy. It does not matter which
angle you come from. And you know what? We don't hear these
arguments every day. They somehow get set aside because those
who believe them are labeled right-wing nuts. The truth is set
aside. It is a very hard thing to know how to respond when you
have the government singing, "Holy, Holy, Holy", and then
spending the rest of the week allowing the destruction of millions
of children.

EUTHANASIA

I'd like to say a word or two about euthanasia. I think
we're going to have it. I don't know that for certain, but I think it's
going to come to America. Turn with me in your Bible to Genesis
Chapter 9 and Exodus Chapter 20. I have to do this quickly. We
can study this more thoroughly some other time. However, I don't
want to leave this parallel subject of the sanctity of life entirely out
of this message. Genesis 9:6 is the first prohibition against murder
in the Bible. Noah's family was coming off the Ark, and in
Genesis 9:6 God tells Noah, "Whosoever sheds man's blood, by
man his blood shall be shed." Then the reason given for the
prohibition of murder is the sacredness of all human life created in
the image of God. *"For in the image of God, He made man."*
Exodus 20 verse 13 is the place in the Bible where you find the
commandment that we all know, *"Thou shalt not kill"* or *"thou
shalt not murder."* To be very brief, I understand that given a
perfect world, with perfect families, perfect doctors, perfect
government, and perfect diagnosis of illnesses, we might know
when a person is going to die. I do not think that euthanasia would
have to be as morally wicked as homicide, but it is in the same
category. If it is not to the same degree as wrong, it is the same

direction. It is like saying I can steal anything because I am poor and in need. Therefore, I can break the commandment against stealing because I have special needs that other people don't have. Breaking God's clear moral law would be a disaster on a societal level.

Doctors make mistakes.

Here are some brief thoughts of the dangers of euthanasia. Number one. Doctors make mistakes. No doctor is infallible. Marilyn Waterhouse's uncle was diagnosed as terminally ill. He was still alive twenty years later. "So, old man, you're done. It's over with." Then he lives decades longer! God is God. Physicians aren't. If euthanasia is practiced, many premature deaths will occur.

The second thing I'd like to say is, "The love of money is the root of all evil" (1 Timothy 6:10). God help us when it becomes profitable to put people out of the way because it will save the government money, it will save the hospital money, it will save the insurance company money, and it will save the family money. God help us.

Thirdly, who decides? We can't trust any of the options. Who decides? Dr. Kevorkian said that doctors ought to decide, not the government. In Holland, where euthanasia is permitted, families can go to the emergency room and find their loved one is already put under. The doctors don't always feel obligated to ask the family. Shall we trust the government to decide cases in which it is financially beneficial for it to cause death? By the way, do you trust all the red tape coming out of the government to be correct? Even if there is integrity, much bungling takes place. People would die from administrative errors. We can't trust the government to make the right decision on life or death. Next, we could let family members decide life or death for an ill relative.

Every relative in the world would choose with wisdom or morality, right? We all know many families would dispatch a relative to cut costs or obtain an inheritance.

Whom do you trust?

Perhaps the patient alone ought to decide. Maybe the patient is the right one. That seems to be the best of the alternatives, but decisions are not made very well when we're in the pit of depression or pain or fear. Decisions are not made well when we're going through the proverbial knothole. All kinds of people, if they have two weeks of excruciating pain, would love to end it all; but if they were able to recover after two weeks, they'd have the rest of their lives. Now, if we give them the option of death in the middle of suffering, many will choose to die needlessly. I'm arguing philosophically here, but in truth no one can be trusted with the decision to end life. At the most, we could withdraw medical treatment and allow death, but actively causing death will cause many avoidable deaths. I still think the Bible alone answers the debate. We are going to have a terrible time if the Supreme Court rules the wrong way on euthanasia. We are going to have moral madness.

Choose you this day whom you will serve.

We have to decide whether we are going to trust God with our lives or whether we're going to be autonomous. Authority over life is the underlying issue. In the case of abortion, will I run my sexuality my own way? Or will I submit my life to God? In the case of euthanasia, will I decide how I will end my life, or will I trust God when I am severely sick? It comes down to an issue of authority whether the master is the individual or God. God is very clear in what He says about the sanctity of life whether in youth or old age.

Let us pray together please. Father, we are saddened by our times. We feel powerless to reverse it. Lord, make us content with what we can do. Make us committed to do what we are able to do in terms of governing our own lives, in terms of influencing families and neighbors, co-workers, and people within the church. We pray for Your mercy in the tough situations, and we pray that all of us will decide to trust Your authority and in Your Son, the Lord Jesus Christ, as our own personal Savior from sin. Bless us as we go our separate ways and may we all feel that we have served You and not have any guilt about being negligent. Thank You, in Jesus Name, Amen.

SUICIDE PREVENTION/
PASTORAL CARE
FOR
DEATH AND BEREAVEMENT

Useful texts;
Suicide, Terminal Illness,
Comfort After a Death

SUICIDE PREVENTION/
PASTORAL CARE
FOR
DEATH AND BEREAVEMENT

Pastoral Care for Potential Suicide

Long term

After stabilization, suicide issues become a sub-section of depression. Detailed studies on depression are found beginning on page 17.

Crisis Period

Practical issues may involve permission for an assistant to remove guns and drugs. A physician may help with a prescription that makes one sleep for a few days and/or restores a rational thinking process. Churches are not equipped for 24-hour supervision. Medical care often allows restored thought that can receive pastoral counsel.

Suicide is fundamentally selfishness. One thinks of only his own problems not the impact of suicide upon others. God has also been forgotten (at least the true God). One might review the attributes and perfections of the Father, the Savior, the Holy Spirit, and the Bible. Attention should be diverted from self and self's problems to thoughts of God's perfections. Some feel their relationship with God is beyond hope. A comparison between Judas and Peter helps. Judas betrayed, Peter denied. Judas killed himself. Peter became one of the greatest Christian leaders in history. The difference was faith and a restored relationship with a gracious God.

Many people have a false image of God. The real God has magnificent attributes including unconditional love and grace. Attention away from self and placed toward a gracious and perfect God helps. If the person has good family ties, it is good to give attention to others who are important.

Suicidal people are in an emotional pit and cannot see light. Discussions on hope for the future helps, though it might be prudent to observe whether thoughts on heaven cause the reaction of wanting to take a short-cut. Discussion on hope for the earthly future may also help. In general, thoughts on self, problems, and the dark present should be shifted toward God, others, and the future.

There are occasions where an allegedly suicidal person will manipulate others. In one incident a man told his girl friend he would kill himself unless she submitted to fornication. Sin must not be rationalized, and false guilt must not be accepted when counseling fails.

Pastoral Care for Terminal Illness

Focus attention upon the attributes of God and the eternal future. God has all strength when we are weak. God has all knowledge when humans, including dedicated physicians, err in ignorance. God is eternal. We are mortal. Yet, God uses His knowledge and power for us, and shares His eternal life with those who trust His Son. It helps to emphasize the perfections and trustworthiness of the Lord Jesus Christ. We really can turn to no other (John 6:68).

Useful texts for a "death-watch":

- Psalms 23, 34, 46, 121

- "To whom then will you liken Me that I should be his equal?" says the Holy One. Lift up your eyes on high and see who has created these stars, the One who leads forth their host by number, He calls them all by name; because of the greatness of His might and the strength of His power not one of them is missing. Why do you say, O Jacob, and assert O Israel, "My way is hidden from the Lord, and the justice due me escapes the notice of my God?" Do you not know? Have you not heard? The Everlasting God, the Lord, the Creator of the ends of the earth does not become weary or tired. His understanding is inscrutable. He gives strength to the weary, and to him who lacks might He increases power. Though youths grow weary and tired, and vigorous young men stumble badly, yet those who wait for the Lord will gain new strength; they will mount up with wings like eagles, they will run and not get tired, they will walk any not become weary [Isa. 40:25-31].

- Do not fear, for I am with you; do not anxiously look about you, for I am your God. I will strengthen you, surely I will help you, surely I will uphold you with my righteous right hand [Isa. 41:10].

- For this reason I say to you, do not be anxious for your life, as to what you shall eat, or what you shall drink; nor for your body, as to what you shall put on. Is not life more than food, and the body than clothing? Look at the birds of the air, that they do not sow, neither do they reap, nor gather into barns, and yet your heavenly Father feeds them. Are you not worth much more than they? And which of you being anxious can add a single cubit to his life's span? And why are you

anxious about clothing? Observe how the lilies of the field
grow; they do not toil nor do they spin, Yet I say to you that
even Solomon in all his glory did not clothe himself like one of
these. But if God so arrays the grass of the field, which is alive
today and tomorrow is thrown into the furnace, will He not
much more do so for you, O men of little faith? Do not be
anxious then, saying, "what shall we eat", or "what shall we
drink?" Or, "with what shall we clothe ourselves?" For all
these things the gentiles eagerly seek; for your heavenly Father
knows that you need all these things. But seek first His
kingdom and His righteousness; and all these things shall be
added to you. Therefore do not be anxious for tomorrow; for
tomorrow will care for itself. Each day has enough trouble of
its own [Matt. 6:25-34].

• And we know that God causes all things to work
together for good to those who love God, to those who are
called according to His purpose. For whom He foreknew, He
also predestined to become conformed to the image of His
Son, that He might be the firstborn among many brethren; and
whom He predestined, these He also called; and whom He
called, these He also justified; and whom He justified, these
He also glorified. What then shall we say to these things? If
God is for us, who is against us? He who did not spare His
own Son, but delivered Him up for us all, how will He not also
with Him freely give us all things? Who will bring a charge
against God's elect? God is the One who justifies; who is the
one who condemns? Christ Jesus is He who died, yes, rather
who was raised, who is at the right hand of God, who also
intercedes for us. Who shall separate us from the love of
Christ? Shall tribulation, or distress, or persecution, or famine,
or nakedness, or peril, or sword? Just as it is written, "For thy
sake we are being put to death all day long; we were
considered as sheep to be slaughtered." But in all things we
overwhelmingly conquer through Him who loved us. For I am
convinced that neither death, nor life, nor angels, nor

principalities, nor things present, nor things to come, nor powers, nor height, nor depth, nor any other created thing, shall be able to separate us from the love of God, which is in Christ Jesus our Lord [Rom. 8:28-39].

"Heaven-texts" are appropriate if the sick person and family have acceptance of death (John 14; 1 Thessalonians 4, 1 Corinthians 15 and so forth).

If the person is too sick for extensive reading, word pictures are effective (God as a refuge, rock, Jesus as a shepherd, the heavenly city or "throne"). Often it is best to use a few basic texts on multiple visits than extensive readings or discussions on deep philosophical questions. The patient's own comments are the best clue in finding pertinent topics. If he or she wants to talk about the meaning of suffering, it is fine to review the material herein (see pages 1-15), but it must be generally applied. The precise reason God might allow a specific person to suffer is a matter between that individual and God.

James 1:17 tells us the only good in this world comes from God. Good blessings that endure forever include the souls of our family/friends and the Bible. There is nothing inherently good in this world. Believers who die go to the source of good.

Obviously, in situations involving an unbeliever, the message that faith in Christ saves us should be given.

Useful texts for loved ones who may be present at the moment of death

We want to give serious attention to the one who just died, but also to think about the scene in another place, heaven.

• Throne room images - Isaiah 6; Revelation 5

• Heavenly city - John 14; Rev. 21:1-5

• Hope for survivors - Psalm 34, 121

• Now it came about that the poor man died and he was carried away by the angels to Abraham's bosom... [Luke 16:22].

• Trust even if one doesn't immediately understand (Prov. 3:5,6).

A Reminder

Whether removal of life support, a gruesome accident scene, a plane crash, a child's death, GO! The pastor represents God, a "no-show" suggests that God has also withdrawn. Go, even if you have no idea what to say.

Pastoral Care for Comfort After a Death

These selections are useful for reading with family and friends in private or for a funeral service.

The Frailty of Life

• As for man, his days are like grass; as a flower of the field, so he flourishes [Psa. 103:15].

• Lord, make me to know my end, and what is the extent of my days, let me know how transient I am. Behold, You have made my days as handbreadths, and my lifetime as nothing in Thy sight, surely every man at his best is a mere breath [Psa. 39:4-5].

- Yet you do not know what your life will be like tomorrow. You are just a vapor that appears for a little while and then vanishes away [James 4:14].

- For, all flesh is like grass, and all its glory like the flower of grass. The grass withers, and the flower falls off, but the Word of the Lord abides forever [1 Pet. 1:24-25].

- For we have brought nothing into the world, so we cannot take anything out of it either [1 Tim. 6:7].

- And he said, "naked I came from my mother's womb, and naked I shall return there. The Lord gave and the Lord has taken away. Blessed be the Name of the Lord" [Job 1:21].

- A voice says, "Call out". Then he answered, "what shall I call out?" All flesh is grass, and all its loveliness is like the flower of the field. The grass withers, the flower fades, when the breath of the Lord blows upon it; surely the people are grass. The grass withers, the flower fades, but the word of our God stands forever [Isa. 40:6-8].

- Also, Psalm 90

The Insignificance of Death in the Light of Eternity

- For I consider that the sufferings of this present time are not worthy to be compared with the glory that is to be revealed to us [Rom. 8:18].

- But we have this treasure in earthen vessels, that the surpassing greatness of the power may be of God and not from ourselves; we are afflicted in every way, but not crushed; perplexed, but not despairing; persecuted, but not forsaken;

struck down, but not destroyed; always carrying about in the body the dying of Jesus, that the life of Jesus may also be manifested in our body…. For momentarily, light affliction is producing for us an eternal weight of glory far beyond all comparison, while we look not at the things that are seen, but at the things that are not seen; for the things that are seen are temporal, but the things that are not seen are eternal [2 Cor. 4:7-10, 17-18].

• And I heard a voice from heaven, saying, "write, 'blessed are the dead who die in the Lord from now on!' " "Yes", says the Spirit, "that they may rest from their labors, for their deeds follow with them" [Rev. 14:13].

Death's Defeat

• Since then the children share in flesh and blood, He himself likewise also partook of the same, that through death He might render powerless him who had the power of death, that is, the devil; and might deliver those who through fear of death were subject to slavery all their lives [Heb. 2:14-15].

• O death, where is your victory? O death, where is your sting? The sting of death is sin, and the power of sin is the law; but thanks be to God, who gives us the victory through our Lord Jesus Christ [1 Cor. 15:55-57].

• [T]hough I walk through the valley of the shadow of death, I fear no evil; for Thou art with me; Thy rod and staff, they comfort me [Psa. 23:4].

A Person's Days are Numbered

• Thine eyes have seen my unformed substance; and in Thy book they were all written, the days that were ordained for me, when as yet there was not one of them [Psa. 139:16].

• Since his days are determined, the number of his months is with Thee, and his limits Thou hast set so that he cannot pass [Job 14:5].

The Intermediate State of Believers in the Lord Jesus Christ (The time after death but before end-time resurrection).

• For we know that if the earthly tent which is our house is torn down, we have a building from God, a house not made with hands, eternal in the heavens. For indeed in this house we groan, longing to be clothed with our dwelling from heaven; inasmuch as we, having put it on, shall not be found naked. For indeed while we are in this tent, we groan, being burdened, because we do not want to be unclothed, but to be clothed, in order that what is mortal may be swallowed up by life. Now He who prepared us for this very purpose is God, who gave to us the Spirit as a pledge. Therefore, being always of good courage, and knowing that while we are at home in the body we are absent from the Lord – for we walk by faith, not by sight – we are of good courage, I say, and prefer rather to be absent from the body and to be at home with the Lord. Therefore also we have as our ambition, whether at home or absent, to be pleasing to Him. For we must all appear before the judgment seat of Christ, that each one may be recompensed for his deeds in the body, according to what he has done, whether good or bad [2 Cor. 5:1-10].

• But I am hard pressed from both directions, having the desire to depart and be with Christ, for that is very much better [Phil. 1:23].

• When the Lamb had broke the fifth seal, I saw underneath the altar the souls of those who had been slain because of the word of God, and because of the testimony which they had maintained; and they cried out with a loud voice, saying, "How long, O Lord, holy and true, wilt Thou refrain from judging and avenging our blood on those who dwell upon the earth" [Rev. 6:9-10].

The Resurrection of Believers

• Even after my skin is destroyed, yet from my flesh I shall see God [Job 19:26].

• But Jesus answered and said unto them, "you are mistaken, not understanding the Scriptures, nor the power of God. For in the resurrection they neither marry, nor are given in marriage, but are like angels in heaven. But regarding the resurrection of the dead, have you not read that which was spoken to you by God, saying, 'I am the God of Abraham, and the God of Isaac, and the God of Jacob'? He is not the God of the dead but of the living" [Matt. 22:29-32] See also Mark 12:24-27.

• Truly, truly I say to you, an hour is coming and now is, when the dead shall hear the voice of the Son of God; and those who hear shall live. For just as the Father has life in Himself, even so He gave to the Son also to have life in Himself; and He gave Him authority to execute judgment, because He is the Son of Man. Do not marvel at this; for an hour is coming, in which all who are in the tombs shall hear His voice, and shall come forth; those who did the good deeds to a resurrection of life, those who committed the evil deeds to a resurrection of judgment [John 5:25-29]

• Jesus said to her, "I am the resurrection and the life; he who believes in Me will live even if he dies, and everyone who lives and believes in Me will never die. Do you believe this?" [John 11:25, 26].

• Behold I tell you a mystery; we shall not all sleep, but we shall all be changed, in a moment, in the twinkling of an eye, at the last trumpet; for the trumpet will sound, and the dead will be raised imperishable, and we shall be changed. For this perishable must put on the imperishable, and this mortal must put on immortality. But when this perishable will have put on the imperishable, and this mortal will have put on immortality, then will come about the saying that is written, "Death is swallowed up in victory. O death, where is your victory? O death, where is your sting?" The sting of death is sin, and the power of sin is the law; but thanks be to God, who gives us the victory through our Lord Jesus Christ. Therefore, my beloved brethren, be steadfast, immovable, always abounding in the work of the Lord, knowing that your toil is not in vain in the Lord [1 Cor. 15:51-58].

• For our citizenship is in heaven, from which also we eagerly await for a Savior, the Lord Jesus Christ; who will transform the body of our humble state into conformity with the body of His glory, by the exertion of the power that He has even to subject all things to Himself [Phil. 3:20-21].

• But we do not want you to be uninformed, brethren, about those who are asleep, that you may not grieve, as do the rest who have no hope. For if we believe that Jesus died and rose again, even so God will bring with Him those who have fallen asleep in Jesus. For this we say to you by the Word of the Lord, that we who are alive, and remain until the coming of the Lord, shall not precede those who have fallen asleep. For the Lord Himself will descend from heaven with a shout, with the voice of the archangel, and with the trumpet of God; and the dead in Christ shall rise first. Then we who are alive and remain shall be caught up together with them in the clouds to meet the Lord in the air, and thus we shall always be with the Lord, Therefore comfort one another with these words [1 Thess. 4:13-18].

• Beloved, now we are the children of God, and it has not appeared as yet what we shall be. We know that, when He appears, we shall be like Him, because we shall see Him just as He is [1 John 3:2].

• Blessed and holy is the one who has a part in the first resurrection; over these the second death has no power, but they will be priests of God and of Christ and will reign with Him for a thousand years [Rev. 20:6].

Heaven and Reunion

• But we do not want you to be uninformed, brethren, about those who are asleep, that you may not grieve, as do the rest who have no hope. For if we believe that Jesus died and rose again, even so God will bring with Him those who have fallen asleep in Jesus. For this we say to you by the Word of the Lord, that we who are alive, and remain until the coming of the Lord, shall not precede those who have fallen asleep. For the Lord Himself will descend from heaven with a shout, with the voice of the archangel, and with the trumpet of God; and the dead in Christ shall rise first. Then we who are alive and remain shall be caught up together with them in the clouds to meet the Lord in the air, and thus we shall always be with the

Lord. Therefore comfort one another with these words [1 Thess. 4:13-18].

• Let not your heart be troubled; believe in God, believe also in me. In my Father's house are many dwelling places; if it were not so, I would have told you; for I go to prepare a place for you. And if I go and prepare a place for you, I will come again, and receive you to Myself, that where I am, there you may be also. And you know the way I am going. Thomas said to Him, "Lord, we do not know where You are going, how do we know the way?" Jesus said to him, "I am the way, and the truth, and the life; no one comes to the Father, but through Me" [John 14:1-6].

• And I saw the holy city, new Jerusalem, coming down out of heaven from God, made ready as a bride adorned for her husband. And I heard a loud voice from the throne saying, "Behold, the tabernacle of God is among men, and He shall dwell among them, and they shall be His people, and God Himself shall be among them, and He shall wipe away every tear from their eyes; and there shall no longer be any death; there shall no longer be any mourning, or crying, or pain; the first things have passed away [Rev. 21:2-4].

• And he showed me a river of the water of life, clear as crystal, coming from the throne of God and of the Lamb, in the middle of its street. And on either side of the river was the tree of life, bearing twelve kinds of fruit, yielding its fruit every month; and the leaves of the tree were for the healing of the nations. And there shall no longer be any curse; and the throne of God and of the Lamb shall be in it, and His bondservants shall serve Him; and they shall see His face, and His name shall be on their foreheads. And there shall no longer be any night; and they shall not have need of the light of a lamp nor the light of the sun, because the Lord God shall illumine them; and they shall reign forever and ever [Rev. 22:1-5].

Worry and Loneliness

God's Peace

• The steadfast of mind Thou wilt keep in perfect peace, because he trusts in Thee [Isa. 26:3].

• Let not your heart be troubled; believe in God, believe also in Me....Peace I leave with you; My peace I give to you; not as the world gives, Do I give to you. Let not your heart be troubled, nor let it be fearful [John 14:1, 27].

• Be anxious for nothing, but in everything by prayer and supplication with thanksgiving let your requests be known to God [Phil. 4:6].

God's Love, Care and Protection – (See also Psalm 23, 121).

• I sought the Lord, and He answered me, and delivered me from all my fears....This poor man cried and the Lord heard him, and saved him out of all his troubles. The angel of the Lord encamps around those who fear Him, and rescues them. O taste and see that the Lord is good; how blessed is the man who takes refuge in Him [Psa. 34:4, 6-8].

• Cast your burden upon the Lord, and He will sustain you; He will never allow the righteous to be shaken [Psa. 55:22].

• Like a shepherd He will tend His flock, in His arm He will gather the lambs, and carry them in His bosom; He will gently lead the nursing ewes [Isa. 40:11].

• For this reason I say to you, do not be anxious for your life, as to what you shall eat, or what you shall drink; nor for your body, as to what you shall put on. Is not life more than food, and the body than clothing? Look at the birds of the air, that they do not sow, neither do they reap, nor gather into barns, and yet your heavenly Father feeds them. Are you not worth much more than they? And which of you being anxious can add a single cubit to his life's span? And why are you anxious about clothing? Observe how the lilies of the field grow; they do not toil nor do they spin, yet I say to you that even Solomon in all his glory did not clothe himself like one of these. But if God so arrays the grass of the field, which is alive today and tomorrow is thrown into the furnace, will He not much more do so for you, O men of little faith? Do not be anxious then, saying, "what shall we eat, or what shall we drink?" Or "with what shall we clothe ourselves?" For all these things the gentiles eagerly seek; for your heavenly Father knows that you need all these things [Matt. 6:25-32].

• Come to Me, all who are weary and heavy laden, and I will give you rest. Take My yoke upon you, and learn from me, for I am gentle and humble in heart; and you shall find rest for your souls. For My yoke is easy, and My load is light [Matt. 11:28-30].

• "Truly, truly I say to you, he who does not enter by the door into the fold of the sheep, but climbs up some other way, he is a thief and a robber. But he who enters by the door is a shepherd of the sheep. To him the doorkeeper opens, and the sheep hear his voice, and he calls his own sheep by name and leads them out. When he puts forth all his own, he goes ahead of them, and the sheep follow him because they know his voice. A stranger they simply will not follow, but will flee from him, because they do not know the voice of strangers". This figure of speech Jesus spoke to them, but they did not understand what those things were which he had been saying to them. So Jesus said to them again, "Truly, truly, I say to you, I am the door of the sheep. All who came before Me are thieves and robbers, but the sheep did not hear them. I am the door; if anyone enters through Me he will be saved, and will go in and out and find pasture. The thief comes only to steal and kill and destroy; I came that they might have life, and have it abundantly. I am the good shepherd; the good shepherd lays down his life for the sheep. He who is a hired hand, and not a shepherd, who is not the owner of the sheep, sees the wolf coming, and leaves the sheep and flees, and the wolf snatches them and scatters them. He flees because he is a hired hand and is not concerned about the sheep. I am the good shepherd, and I know My own and My own know Me, even as the Father knows me and I know the Father; and I lay down my life for the sheep. I have other sheep, which are not of this fold; I must bring them also, and they will hear my voice; and they will become one flock with one shepherd. For this reason the Father loves Me, because I lay down My life so that I may take it again. No one has taken it away from Me, but I lay it down on My own initiative. I have authority to lay it down, and I have authority to take it up again. This commandment I received from My Father....and I give eternal life to them, and they will never perish; and no one will snatch them out of My hand. My Father, who has given them to Me, is greater than all; and no one is able to snatch them out of the Father's hand. I and the Father are one." [John 10:1-18, 28-30].

• And we know that God causes all things to work together for good to those who love God, to those who are called according to His purpose....What then shall we say to these things? If God is for us, who is against us....But in all these things we overwhelmingly conquer through Him who loved us. For I am convinced that neither death, nor life, nor angels, nor principalities, nor things present, nor things to come, nor powers, nor height, nor depth, nor any other created thing, shall be able to separate us from the love of God, which is in Christ Jesus our Lord Rom. 8:28, 31, 37-39].

• [C]asting all your anxiety on Him, because He cares for you [1 Pet. 5:7].

• Make sure that your character is free from the love of money, being content with what you have; for He Himself has said, "I will never desert you, nor will I ever forsake you" [Heb. 13:5].

God's Strength (See also Psalm 91).

• Have I not commanded you? Be strong and courageous. Do not tremble or be dismayed, for the Lord your God is with you wherever you go [Josh. 1:9].

• Behold, how happy is the man whom God reproves, so do not despise the discipline of the Almighty. For He inflicts pain, and gives relief; He wounds, and His hands also heal. From six troubles He will deliver you, even in seven evil will not touch you [Job 5:17-19].

• God is our refuge and strength, a very present help in trouble....cease striving and know that I am God; I will be exalted among the nations, I will be exalted in the earth. The Lord of hosts is with us; the God of Jacob is our stronghold....[Psa. 46:1, 10,11].

• Do you not know? Have you not heard? The everlasting God, the Lord, the Creator of the ends of the earth does not become weary or tired. His understanding is inscrutable. He gives strength to the weary, and to him who lacks might He increases power. Though youths grow weary and tired, and vigorous young men stumble badly, yet those who wait for the Lord will gain new strength; they will mount up with wings like eagles, they will run and not get tired, they will walk and not become weary [Isa. 40:28-31].

• Do not fear, for I am with you; do not anxiously look about you, for I am your God. I will strengthen you, surely I will help you, surely I will uphold you with My righteous right hand [Isa. 41:10].

• The Lord is good, a stronghold in the day of trouble, and He knows those who take refuge in Him [Nahum 1:7].

Direction

• I will instruct you and teach you in the way which you should go; I will counsel you with My eye upon you [Psa. 32:8].

• Trust in the Lord with all your heart, and do not lean on your own understanding. In all your ways acknowledge Him, and He will make your paths straight [Prov. 3:5-6].

Counting Blessings

• Consider it all joy, my brethren, when you encounter various trials, knowing that the testing of your faith produces endurance. And let endurance have its perfect result, that you may be perfect and complete, lacking in nothing [James 1:2-4].

Also, Psalm 103:1-18

Joy

• Rejoice in the Lord always; again I say rejoice! Let your forbearing spirit be known to all men. The Lord is near. Be anxious for nothing, but in everything by prayer and supplication with thanksgiving let your requests be made known unto God. And the peace of God, which surpasses all comprehension, shall guard your hearts and your minds in Christ Jesus. Finally, brethren, whatever is true, whatever is honorable, whatever is right, whatever is pure, whatever is lovely, whatever is of good repute, if there is any excellence and if anything worthy of praise, let your mind dwell on these things. The things you have learned and received and heard and seen in me, practice these things, and the God of peace shall be with you [Phil. 4:4-9].

• Until now you have asked for nothing in My Name; ask, and you will receive, that your joy may be made full [John 16:24].

• And these things we write, so that our joy may be made complete [1 John 1:4].

Faith

• Commit your way to the Lord, trust also in Him, and He will do it [Psa. 37:5].

• When I am afraid, I will put my trust in Thee. In God, whose word I praise. In God have I put my trust; I shall not be afraid. What can mere man do to me? [Psa. 56:3-4].

•Trust in the Lord with all you heart, and do not lean on your own understanding. In all your ways acknowledge Him, and He will make your paths straight [Prov. 3:5-6].

Death is not "natural". The Word of God calls it the "last enemy" (1 Cor. 15:26), and says only Christ has power to defeat death. Again, at the time of bereavement, we have no other place to go. Peter said, "Lord, to whom shall we go? You have the words of eternal life" (John 6:68). Those in bereavement need reminder and reassurance that the truth of the preceding verses come not from a pastor, a church, or a denomination. The Lord Jesus Christ is the Savior with such otherwise unbelievable promises. He has the power to keep them and would never lie to us about such serious issues. After the guarantee of a heavenly home, He also said, "if it were not so I would have told you" (John 14:2).

FAMILIES
OF
THE MENTALLY ILL

This section includes two essays on families of the
mentally ill and a compilation of letters received by
Westcliff Bible Church from families with a mentally ill
member. All three papers were presented by Dr. Waterhouse
for a panel on mental illness at the world conference of the
American Association of Christian Counselors

Families
of
the Mentally Ill

In the middle of the night my brother started screaming in the next bedroom. He fought with non-existent people only he could see and hear. He ripped the light fixture from the ceiling and pulled at the wires, all the time telling the voices to go away. Our family really began to be worried when he ripped up a Bible and smashed a praying-hands wall plaque. Mark had been the co-captain of our high school football and basketball teams. We attended a fine church with a fine pastor. Yet, at age seventeen he unraveled mentally. At low points he would stand before a mirror and laugh, unable to follow a conversation. His old personality was lost and remains so to this day. The state mental hospital diagnosed schizophrenia. They did every imaginable medical test and eliminated drug abuse. Despite a common perception among Christians that severe mental problems arise from bad parenting or from deep sins, we knew our family to be healthy. Of course, we are fallen; but Mom and Dad have now been married for more than fifty years. With the same parental philosophy one son has schizophrenia. The other has written a theology book. One son lives in a home for the mentally ill, improved but not cured. The other pastors a church. Our family rejected the view that mental illness stems from drug abuse or dysfunctional homes (though one can obviously find dual-diagnosis examples where a person has more than one problem).

I wondered about demonic influence when I saw my brother shouting at invisible beings and tearing up a Bible. However, Mark believes in Christ and has no interest in the occult. Regardless of the debate over whether a Christian might be possessed, it is a fair Scriptural conclusion that Christ's power protects believers from involuntary seizure by demons. Furthermore, knowledge of schizophrenia reveals differences from biblical accounts of demons. Demons spoke in complete sentences in rational dialogue. Untreated people with schizophrenia tend to speak in "word salads." They ramble with little direction to the conversation. Demon possessed people want nothing to do with Christ…"What business do we have with each other…?" (Matt. 8:29). Mental patients often seek spiritual help. Mental hospital chaplains often find receptivity to the gospel and to Christian counseling after thought processes have been stabilized medically. After deliverance, the demoniac was "in his right mind" (Mark 5:15). This may only mean he was no longer suicidal or violent. There may not be any reference to mental illness. However, even if we infer that demons can cause mental illness, we also know demons cause blindness, deafness, muteness, and epilepsy. It would be ignorant and cruel to tell all people with blindness and epilepsy they are demon-possessed. Likewise, we cannot glibly diagnose demonic causation of the two million cases in America with schizophrenia.

Adoption studies from Oregon, Denmark, and Israel show schizophrenia runs in families even if children are raised by adoptive parents and not a biological parent who has mental illness. The closer blood ties one has to a person with schizophrenia, the greater the risk for developing the disorder. Identical twins have a 48% risk. Children have a 13% risk. Siblings have a 9% risk. The general population only has a 1% risk.

Nothing in Scripture contradicts the conclusion that severe mental illness stems from a medical problem. The Bible presents Nebuchadnezzar's example of an extremely rare mental illness where one believes himself to be an animal. Moses warns Israel that "madness" might be one of the curses for apostasy (Deut. 28:28). The other curses in the context are all medical problems implying that "madness" is also a medical problem. God also warned of blindness, boils, tumors, scabs, and incurable itching (v. 27). No one would generalize from this Scripture that all cases of boils or tumors show God's wrath. Why should we single out mental illness and conclude it alone is always God's punishment? Any medical problem could be chastisement, but a universal conclusion about chastisement for schizophrenia would be just as foolish as one for blindness (John 9:2-3).

When evangelicals understand the problem of mental illness, then God's Word can be applied with wisdom, and great ministry results. At the time of psychiatric crisis a church may not be able to minister in any comprehensive way to the patient. I find a parallel with ministry to those in a coma. Intensive care does not lend itself to deep Bible study. Nevertheless, how would a family respond if no one visited a relative in a coma? The critical factor at a time of psychiatric meltdown is that a church overcomes awkwardness and stigma and proves its love even if the situation does not lend itself to human control. The tendency is for churches to withdraw. At the same time a family facing a loved ones mental illness tends to be so exhausted and stigmatized that it withdraws from church. This cycle has led many families to drop out of church and wonder why pastors do not care. At the time of hospitalization, ministry may not involve complex strategies, but the church needs to preserve relationships for a better day. Prayer, giving Bible promises, and loving interest, all prove that Christians care about needs, even the kind we cannot quickly fix. Resulting bonds often enable more extensive ministry over time.

A psychiatrist said, "I can tune the piano, but only God can make music again." When mentally ill people have their thinking "tuned" by medical care, many of them can later benefit from Bible truth. Yet, from the beginning, churches must remember to include the entire family within the domain of ministry. We would not overlook the spouse, siblings, children, and extended family members of those with any other illness comparable in severity.

Many genuinely want to help but do not know how. The most important factor in giving an answer is understanding a problem. The Bible is indeed the source for prescribing spiritual answers to life. However, Christians have been poor in describing the exact nature of mental illness and its devastating emotional and spiritual impact upon a home. With more accurate descriptions of family needs, it becomes clear the Bible gives relevant prescriptions. Those who think Christianity must defer all areas of help for schizophrenia to medical experts are wrong. The truth that schizophrenia is a complex medical problem need not prevent ministry. We refuse to let other complex medical problems become a barrier to ministry.

Medicine is necessary but not sufficient. A reporter once pushed a microphone at me and asked, "What do conservative Christians believe about mental health professionals?" I said, "They are necessary for medicine and suicide prevention. They are not sufficient to give the abundant life. Only faith in Christ and the Bible can give full treatment for mental illness."

Families experience guilt, often legitimate guilt, over harsh treatment. Mentally ill people can exhibit behaviors that cause relatives to snap back with harshness. Families, especially parents, feel false guilt over thinking they have caused mental illness. God specializes in guilt therapy. Faith in Christ as Savior solves guilt before God as Judge. After salvation, confession of sin solves guilt before God as Father. 1 John 3:20 helps with false guilt "...in whatever our heart condemns us...God is greater than our heart and knows all things."

Families of the mentally ill experience isolation and types of fears unknown to others. Christian friends can prevent loneliness. God's Word contains many promises concerning fears (Psalm 55:22; John 14:1, 27; Phil. 4:6-9; 1 John 4:18; 1 Peter 5:7). These families live with fear (violence, suicide, side-effects of psychiatric drugs, another child developing schizophrenia, finances, stigma, lost dreams of a child's personality and potential to succeed). One half of families report worry about their relative becoming a missing person. I personally know a Christian ophthalmologist who lost a son for ten years, and a pastor whose missing son died on the streets.

In addition to helping with guilt, loneliness, and fears, a church might offer these families counseling for marital stress and depression. A pastor or counselor may be needed for complex problems. However, in our specialized world we must not disparage the value of simply being a true friend.

The Bible addresses the emotions faced by families of the mentally ill. It also answers their theological questions. What good can come from suffering? Suffering can result in dependence upon God, humility, sympathy, credibility for ministry, opportunities for evangelism, increased Bible study and prayer, unity, and spiritual endurance. Just as in Christ's life, we experience suffering before glory, the cross before the crown. What is the value of a person who will not succeed in life? He or she may never marry, finish school or get rich. We need to remind these families that all people are created in God's image. The *sanctity of life* extends to those with mental illness. Believers with mental illness remain children of God, clothed in Christ's righteousness. Ministry to families of the mentally ill must reinforce God's unconditional love and the worth of people who too often are viewed as modern leper equivalents.

A church in Kansas City worked with a mental hospital chaplain to invite families of the mentally ill to a banquet. They used real silver and linen tablecloths to create an atmosphere conveying value. Another church in California employed a retired music teacher to form a bell choir in which all participants have schizophrenia. By having a part in church life and by traveling to other churches, these musicians feel more useful to God, and the public has more understanding and less fear of those treated for mental illness.

Christian colleges should begin welcoming chapel speeches and special lectures on mental illness. Future Christian workers need not become experts on psychiatric issues, but awareness and an adequate description of the need is essential. We are also uninformed about all current attitudes in secular psychiatry; this must be corrected as well.

Antipathy between psychiatry and Christianity exists but has waned since Freudian days. E. Fuller Torrey, today's world leader on schizophrenia, endorses the ministry of Westcliff Bible Church and tells his readers churches should be "natural allies" in helping families of the mentally ill.

Hollywood awarded a movie on schizophrenia, *A Beautiful Mind*, with ample reason. Schizophrenia alone accounts for 40% of all long term hospital beds. It concerns the work of an astonishing number of society's leaders, not just physicians, nurses, and social workers, but politicians, judges, teachers, policeman, and clergy. Some professionals will study a Bible-based book on mental illness when they would never touch Christian books on other contemporary issues. Indirectly, they then encounter the gospel. No religious background prevents families from seeking Biblical help. Requests for information on Westcliff Bible Church's *Ministry to the Families of the Mentally Ill* have come from Catholics, Orthodox, Mormons, Jews, and Protestants from fundamentalist to liberal in sixty nations, mostly through word-of-mouth publicity.

It is unfortunate that the Christian community does not yet regard the two million families of the mentally ill as a target group for evangelism like other sub-cultures such as prisoners or international students. In reality this population comprises one of the great fields ripe for harvest. The gospel finds greatest welcome among those with hopeless problems.

When evangelicals finally do understand this need, then we will wonder how we ever thought Christianity had so little to contribute in the way of ministry. When silence over mental illness ends, churches will discover families of the mentally ill in their congregations. When we remember that pain often results in a search for God, we will think of families of the mentally ill as a ministry that we can no longer ignore.

THE CHURCH
AND
MENTAL ILLNESS

Theology prescribes. Psychology describes.

The Bible gives answers for pastoral counseling. But what is the exact problem?

Misdiagnosis of a problem leads to misapplication of the Bible in pastoral counseling. The point may be true, but it will not help if it addresses a problem the person does not have. We must understand mental illness and its impact upon families before giving counsel. Even if a pastor cannot immediately help the person in a crisis, the family remains within the domain of pastoral care at all times. This is true of a one in a coma after a car accident or a psychiatric breakdown. The relationship must be preserved now and help given to the mentally ill person after medical treatment has improved thinking.

Families of people with schizophrenia (2,000,000 families in the United States alone) have been totally overlooked as targets for evangelism. Medical angles for evangelism have been largely ignored but would be more effective than some common methods.

Medical Observations
Schizophrenia runs in family lines. [1]

---

[1]   (see Steven Waterhouse, *Strength For His People*, Amarillo TX: Westcliff Press, 2002, p. 18).

•Adoption studies in Oregon, Denmark, and Israel, establish that family environment is not the critical factor.

•MRI studies show enlarged ventricles in some twin comparisons.

Mental Illness is not a Myth

•Myth: Dysfunctional homes cause it.   No, it also strikes in stable homes.

•Myth: Use of Drugs causes it. Not necessarily. Many mentally ill people have never taken drugs.

•Myth: Defense for a crime - Moral responsibility can be detected when one practices cover-up, blame shifting, and moral indignation when he or she is offended by a sin. Most mentally ill people exhibit such traits of moral responsibility even if it is harder for them to do what is right because of their distorted thinking. Millions of mentally ill people have never been charged with a crime and are not faking it in case they might need a future excuse for one.

•Myth: Divine chastisement or demonic influence - (see discussion, pp. 92-99, and below, p. 177). There may be cases of dual-diagnosis just as mentally ill people might also take drugs, but most of the time demons can be ruled out.

Mental Illness and the Bible

Does the Bible teach all cases of mental illness are chastisement?

♦ Most Bible references to mental illness are false accusations designed to stigmatize or isolate another (David, 1 Sam. 21:12-15; Jesus, Mark 3:21; Paul, Acts 26:24-25).

♦ Nebuchadnezzar, see Daniel Chapter 4. This example may show that God might use mental illness as a chastisement, but we may not generalize Nebuchadnezzar's example to all. Furthermore, the delusion that one is an animal is an extraordinarily rare disorder. It is definitely not a common symptom of schizophrenia.

♦ Deut. 28:27-29, 34 mentions madness as a divine chastisement.

☐ All items in these verses are medical problems (boils, tumors, scabs, blindness). This means "madness" is also a medical problem even if sometimes God uses it to discipline.

☐ If "madness" is one way of chastisement, then the conclusion that an individual case of mental illness is God's chastisement is still no more universally transferable to all than would be boils or tumors. In fact, baldness can be a sign of God's wrath in Scripture. Would we want to make a universal principal that all cases of baldness are chastisement?

☐ No given medical problem is ever a universal sign of God's chastisement. Only deep rebellion in ones life suggests the possibility of chastisement. A definite conclusion that God is disciplining another is almost always a private matter between the afflicted one and the Holy Spirit.

Mental Illness and Demons

Are mentally ill people demon-possessed?

♦ In the New Testament demons spoke in rational dialogue. Untreated people with schizophrenia speak in "word-salads".

♦ Demons have an aversion to Christ. Mentally ill people often want spiritual help.

♦ Demons might give supernatural knowledge to their host. Mentally ill people never exhibit clairvoyance.

♦ Assuming demons to be secretive, we presume those who claim to be demon-possessed are not.

♦ Supernatural phenomena are indications of evil spirits not mental illness.

♦ If medicine alleviates the problems, it was not demons.

♦ In the case of Mark 5:15 the restoration to a "right mind" may only mean the former demoniac was no longer suicidal or violent. There may not be any reference to schizophrenia. If a "right mind" does refer to a healing from insanity, then we still may not view all cases of mental illness as caused by demons. In the New Testament, demons cause epilepsy, deafness, blindness, muteness, and suicidal feelings. No one would seriously want to diagnose demons in all modern cases of these problems.

It is certainly possible that some who are demon-possessed have been misdiagnosed as mentally ill and placed in mental hospitals, but the classic symptoms of schizophrenia are different from New Testament demon possession. (For symptoms of New Testament demon possession see "Demons or Mental Illness", pages 85-99).

Mental Illness and Society

Mental Illness overlaps with the work of an astounding number of leaders (politicians, judges, attorneys, police, teachers, doctors and other medical professionals, chaplains of all kinds [military, hospital, prison], social workers, college professors, and millions of families. Four out of ten long-term hospital beds are taken by schizophrenia alone! The fact that *A Beautiful Mind* won the movie of the year shows society's interest in this problem. Opportunities to evangelize and give attention to the Bible's counsel are great.

Even if medicine is necessary, it is not sufficient for the abundant life. The non-Christian would often realize this. A psychiatrist once said, "I can tune the piano, but only God can teach a mentally ill person to make music again."

Emotional Needs of the Family

The Bible teaches about the emotional needs and philosophical questions faced by families of the mentally ill. Christianity could make a great ministry contribution. When we finally understand the problem, it is not hard to apply the Bible. This is especially true if we do not overlook the families. Even the mentally ill person might benefit from pastoral care after medicine has improved thinking.

Problems and Spiritual Questions Among Families of the Mentally Ill

♦ Guilt of Various Kinds

☐ Some have false guilt over causing a child to become mentally ill (see 1 John 3:20).

□ Some have true guilt over treatment of those with the exasperating behaviors involved in mental illness - 53% in a survey (Waterhouse, 1995) feel guilty over harsh treatment of a relative. Unsaved people need faith in Christ to remove guilt before God as Judge. Believers need confession to remove guilt before God as Father.

♦ Fear - Mental illness in a home causes fears among relatives that other families do not face (50% surveyed worry about their relative becoming lost on the streets, 95% worry about care after parental death, 10% of those with schizophrenia do kill themselves, (see Psa. 55:22; Isa. 41:10, and also *Strength for His People*, pp. 59-61).

♦ Anger - Many are angry with God for allowing the mental breakdown of a relative (40% by survey). The Bible allows respectful venting (even Jesus asked "Why?"). However, we must develop a philosophy of suffering (see Suffering, What Good Is It?, pages 1-15).

♦ Marriage Counseling - A relative's mental illness causes marital disagreements.

♦ Depression - One out of 13 relatives report a suicide attempt because care-giving for a mentally ill person is too tough (See Depression, Biblical Causes and Counseling, pages 17-61).

♦ Stigma, isolation, and loneliness - The worst emotional adjustment arises in families who withdraw from church, though many of them do just that. The combination of shame plus the awkwardness that church leaders have in counseling these families leads to withdrawal from church. They need fellowship.

♦ Questions about suffering (see Suffering, What Good Is It?, pages 1-15) - What good can come from suffering? Why does God allow a terrible disorder like schizophrenia? Why my family?

♦ Questions about human value - What good is a person who will never achieve by societal standards of achievement (marriage, education, career, income)?

♦ Questions about demons - Do demons cause mental illness? What are the voices? Falsely thinking ones relative is demon-possessed causes a poor family response to a relative's mental illness (See also Demons or Mental Illness, pages 81-115).

Summary:

The Bible prescribes answers, but Christian leaders must first describe the exact nature of the problem. Pastors might not be able to help a mentally ill person in a crisis mode, but they can preserve the relationship until stabilization. At all times the families are the responsibility of the church. Once the problem is understood, the Bible has great relevance to the needs and questions among families of the mentally ill. These families comprise a huge, overlooked target group for evangelism, and helping them also brings interaction and ministry with unsaved leaders in many diverse professions. Evangelicals lose opportunities from failing to address this need through awkwardness, ignorance, and withdrawal. In reality, there is a wide open door for potential ministry (Rev. 3:8).

Profile
of Families
of
the Mentally Ill

(Unless qualified, these comments are from letters to Westcliff Bible Church, Amarillo, TX with names withheld, survey statistics from Steven Waterhouse dissertation studies at Dallas Theological Seminary)

Relationships to other Christians

Less than 6% of families of the mentally ill believe pastors give good pastoral care for families of the mentally ill. Almost 60% do not believe Christians care about their needs. Numerous responses indicate families will keep mental illness secret from their pastors or churches.

"Our experience with other Christians, ministers, and family members during this illness was that they were sincerely concerned, but they didn't know what to do or how to help. They really were of very little help."

"There is no other support out there [beyond NAMI, National Alliance for the Mentally Ill]. Psychiatrists just disperse medicine and can't be bothered with quality of life for patient or family. Psychological therapy is blaming! The church is also blaming! Friends desert you! It might be contagious. God is not the problem. He carries you! The church does not equal Christ."

"The church is the first place we were hurt and abandoned....I believe that the stigma of mental illness began

with the 'religious' in the very beginning....Therefore, it is my
opinion, that until the Christian community takes a completely
different stand, society as a whole will not change its mind."

"Both of these surveys assume that a Christian will go
to his/her pastor for counseling. My experiences have taught
me that the pastor is either unavailable for any counseling or
operates from the mind set that if Christians experience serious
troubles, he or she sinned in some way and brought them on....
What a comfort and solace it would be if I had the option of
seeking and receiving Christian counseling from a godly
pastor."

"Due to the stigma of mental illness, I have never
shared my hurt with many people from my church. Especially
pastors!"

Relationships Within the Family

Almost 10% report that stress caused by a relative's
mental illness has led to a divorce (often the parents of a
mentally ill person). Relationships between siblings can also be
strained. Over 90% of the families say they live with stress.

"It is difficult for any family with schizophrenia but
even more so for a pastor's family. The church members
generally do not understand. They tend to be very critical of the
pastor and point the finger at him saying, 'How can he control
others when he can't even straighten out the problems in his
own house!?' "

"Some of my answers are heavily influenced by the
fact that I am raising her 11 year old son born out of wedlock.
She was hospitalized with delusional spirals when Seth was
two years old. The state placed him with us permanently
causing great friction between my sister and me. He was born

with a brain tumor causing permanent hydrocephalism. He has already had 11 shunt revisions while in our care... adding to the stress."

Emotions Experienced by the Family

Guilt

Often families are made to feel guilt for causing a loved ones mental illness. All have sinned, but mental illness is not caused by bad parenting. The following quote from a minister in Georgia illustrates the stigma that can be placed on such families.

"In the early days of my son's illness, the commonly accepted theories of the cause of mental illness emphasized environmental factors such as 'poor parenting' or perhaps 'emotional or physical abuse.' We heard about the 'schizophrenigenic mother' and the 'ineffectual father' and later 'pathological families,' 'identified patients', and 'double binds.' These only increased our guilt, sent us examining ourselves for failures and too often blaming each other. One of the most devastating experiences I have ever experienced was the night a counselor placed two chairs in the middle of the office, instructed me to sit in one and my son in the other and said, 'Now apologize to your son for what you have done to him.' Unfortunately, in spite of recent research, these theories still are widely held. Recently, I was leading an in-service training session at a community mental health center. One staff member stated categorically, 'Families are usually sicker than the patients.' Such attitudes by some mental health professionals have added to the burden of guilt and failure."

Anger

Families of the mentally ill can experience anger at medical professionals, the ill family member, society in general and even God:

"I get to the part in The Lord's Prayer that says, 'Thy will be done', and I think No! Not if this is His will. Why I ask, does God permit such a horrible thing to happen to someone?" (the source here was not a personal letter).

"I wonder how God could do this to me. I haven't been perfect, but I've done the best I could. And I love my wife. But then I think I have no right to question God. For me that is the hardest part. I think I must be a very weak person to question God."

"In a special way I know now [that the] mental illness of our loved one has been a blessing to me from God even though at the onsought [onset] of the illness I would be angry at God at times. There was a time in the first two years of my son's schizophrenia that I decided I would no longer pray because God was seemingly not hearing my prayers, but the situation got worse daily. For a whole week I did not pray, but I could not live without prayer.... Although I know intellectually I was wrong, I felt so hurt by God, so forsaken. How could this happen to my son who was a good Christian and even considered becoming a pastor?"

Fear

Families of the mentally ill encounter types of fear unknown by others. Over 80% fear violence from an unmedicated family member. At least half of parents worry their son or daughter will wander off and become a street person. Close to 100% of parents fear no one will care for a mentally ill child after the parents die."

"There is serious stress in my life as our younger daughter is in Christian therapy to be healed by the devastating violence her older schizophrenic sister perpetrated on her. While we as a family forgave her, violence in our home caused by her has damaged emotionally several of us. For our family, our daughter's violence has been the major source of hurt, fear and concern."

"My sibling has twice been released early or prematurely. She has virtually disappeared and left the state in which she resides. This is causing tremendous stress and worry on the part of my family."

"...Our son is very rebellious, even now the nurses in the hospital he is in do not believe he is taking his medication. He is very violent!"

"My son is in a state prison for the mentally ill after committing a murder.... his mental illness was not accepted by the jury. I as a parent was never asked any questions, and I could not afford a private lawyer."

"It has been 10 years since my sister was diagnosed as schizophrenic. She was then hospitalized but has not been since then.... She lives with two small children (her husband left her). She is especially dependent emotionally and somewhat financially and physically on my elderly parents. I told my mother (sort of as a joke) last year that I was glad she hadn't died because then I would have to take care of my sister. We love her dearly, but she is a burden."

Depression

Taking care of a mentally ill relative can be so stressful that families become depressed. One out of thirteen families report that an immediate family member has attempted suicide because of stress arising from a relative's mental illness. Thirty-five per cent claim they have heard a family member talk of suicide. As for those who have schizophrenia, about 10% commit suicide. On the average, schizophrenia shortens life by 14 years.

"Several times in all of this I very seriously toyed with suicide. I cleaned out possessions, knew how I would do it, etc., and somehow a loving and caring God would give me a vignette on Christian radio - maybe just a verse - and I could go on a step or two."

"....was hospitalized at Kalamazoo State Hospital for 2 years before he succeeded in committing suicide after six serious attempts. Our family has been ravaged by this tragedy. We all loved him very much and cannot understand why God allowed him to suffer so terribly. He was a young man who loved God and his fellow man....it doesn't make any sense. The spiritual struggle is the hardest."

Denial

Nearly 60% of families deny the initial diagnosis of schizophrenia. However, after long-term symptoms exist or perhaps even a second opinion is obtained, reality must be accepted. Mental illness is not a myth.

"In my particular case, I was 33 before I knew that my mother was diagnosed as schizophrenic. The diagnosis was made when I was two years old, but our father and his relatives told us 'that's just how your mother is.' It would hurt when other kids would call her 'crazy,' but we weren't ever told until I forced the issue at age 33. The denial of my father and other relatives made the lives of three small children very confusing and frustrating and didn't help our mother either."

Demons

Demonic possession is both a Biblical and experiential reality. However, the symptoms of schizophrenia can be differentiated from the descriptions of demons in the New Testament. Survey statistics show that the families with the worst emotional adjustments are those with those who have withdrawn from church and those who believe relatives are demon-possessed.

"I hear voices in my head that no one else hears, and I also have paranoid ideas that all the people in San Antonio, Texas have some kind of conspiracy against me. I also believe that it is because of a satanic cult that's putting a hex on me. If there is anything you can do, please write me back."

"I've had a bad experience with a church I used to go to because of my illness. They said I was demon-possessed. It was a painful experience."

"My son became ill with schizophrenia four and a half years ago at the age of 15. My father came out here from California at the time; while I was at work he tried to cast a demon out of my son. He refuses to see my son as having an illness. I have not been able to let my son have contact with his grandfather because he has told me he would continue to tell Tyson that he is demon-possessed. My son loves God and was a good Christian before, as well as, after the onset of schizophrenia."

Overcoming the Pain

With God's help many families actually grow from the painful experience of having a relative with mental illness. Christians have great ministry contributions for their families if we only stop neglecting them and apply the Bible to their specific needs.

"In a special way I now know the mental illness of our loved one has been a blessing to me from God...."

"We found a path to a wonderful Christian life because of our son's illness. We might never have recognized our spiritual needs except for his illness and our need to cope with it."

"If anything, living with the mental illness of our son has caused me more deeper empathy for these sufferers.... has made me a better person.... More was learned from our own experience more humility and genuine caring."

Conclusion

Families of the mentally ill are a large and needy target group for evangelism and Biblical counseling. Evangelistic efforts in secular situations have been fruitful. Churches prepared to minister would prevent members from departing, as well as, find new families. This paper only profiles needs.

Additional resources on how to evangelize or comfort families of the mentally ill may be found in *Strength For His People; A Ministry to families of the Mentally Ill* by Dr. Steven Waterhouse (Available from Westcliff Press, P.O. Box 1521, Amarillo TX 79105, (806) 359-6362, or at Dr. Waterhouses's web site www.webtheology.com, cost $4.00 including postage and handling).

The Word of God makes a counselor or friend "equipped for every good work" (2 Tim. 3:17). Life presents tough questions, "...but the answer of the tongue is from the Lord" (Prov.16:1). We cannot possibly do any better than searching the Scriptures for the answers to our tough questions.

Appendix

LET'S GO BACK
TO
SQUARE ONE

E. Jay O'Keefe

"God is in control, and He has my best interest at heart"

E. Jay O'Keefe

Mr. O'Keefe is a founding elder of Westcliff Bible Church, the congregation that has made it possible to publish Dr. Waterhouse's works. He has degrees from Amarillo College, Texas Tech University, and a Masters degree in Mathematics from the University of Michigan. He is a past President of Western National Life Insurance Company, now owned by AIG. For years he has provided financial counseling and asset management for many. In the 1980s, Mr. O'Keefe taught a seminar on the Biblical principles of handling money. He occasionally fills the pulpit at Westcliff Bible Church; the message of this appendix is the first in a series of messages on what he calls "Square One Theology".

LET'S GO BACK
TO
SQUARE ONE

Some years ago, I was invited to sit in on a Bible class that was being conducted by conference telephone call and involved Christian businessmen in three different cities. The teacher of the class was a former Navigator missionary who had been discipling businessmen for over forty years. During the time I was in this class, I gained a better understanding of some of the great doctrines of our faith, especially how they apply to daily life. As I get older it is these truths that have most dramatically changed my life that I enjoy sharing with others, and occasionally preaching from the pulpit of my church. The truth that I share here is at the top of my list of life-changing truths. It is, therefore, with much enthusiasm that I write this. As I do so I have in my mind in a special way my children and grandchildren. I pray God would use this in their hearts and lives for His glory. I would be pleased if He used it in other lives also.

This truth is not new. It is not a new doctrine. It is the application of an old truth to life, an application I had largely missed during the years I have been a Christian. It has to do with two of God's attributes, His sovereignty and His goodness.

If you enrolled in a seminary as a student, you would sit in a class entitled *Theology Proper*, which is a study of God Himself; His attributes, His nature, His activities, as revealed in

Scripture. Let's say that you do enroll, and you show up for
theology class the first day. The professor begins to list God's
attributes and explain them; sovereignty, goodness, justice,
love, eternal life, omnipotence, and so on. You leave class that
first day with a little better understanding of what God is like.

Now let's suppose two or three days later you
encounter an unexpected crisis in your life, a major problem of
some kind. It is the kind of problem you have to share with
somebody, someone you trust, someone who might act as a
counselor for you. You get with this person and tell him or her
all about your crisis. You come to a pause, and your counselor
looks you in the eye and says, "**Don't you realize that God is
in control and has your best interest at heart?**" And
immediately you think, "is that what I learned in theology class
earlier this week?" Actually it was, but it was presented quite
differently. In theology class you learned it as a *statement* of
theology, or a *statement* of faith. But in the visit with the
counselor, you heard it as the *application* of theology to real
life. If God is sovereign, then **He is in control** of everything,
not just some things. He's in control because He created all
things. To think of God as having created this world, and not
be in control of it, doesn't make sense. That wouldn't be the
God of the Bible. If God is good, absolutely righteous, then He
is **incapable** of doing anything with your life, or letting
anything happen in your life that is not in your best interest.
And hence the phrase, *God is in control and has your best
interest at heart*. This implies that our faith rests on two
foundations, the **sovereignty** of God and the **goodness** of God.
Because of the way this has impacted my life, I call it my
Square One Theology, or simply, *Square One*.

I am learning that **every** issue in life, **every** relationship
in life, **every** experience in life should be approached from the
foundation of *Square One;* "**God is in control and has my**

best interest at heart." As I begin each new day, I try to go to S*quare One,* and start there. I try to affirm my belief in it. I try to reinvest my faith in it. If I fail to do that on a given day, it's a different kind of day. You see, the problem is not in my statement of faith or what I say I believe. The problem is my failure to live consistently with what I say I believe. The problem is **application.**

The great British theologian, Charles Spurgeon, who ministered in the middle and late 1800s in England, taught a concept that he titled "Practical Atheism." He said even though a believer is not an atheist, he can sometimes act like one. He can act as if one or more of God's attributes were not true. Consider an illustration of this that has been helpful to me. Let's suppose you learn the attributes of God in Bible class. Some teachers have divided God's attributes into a series of ten. Let's say you go to the store and you buy ten plaques. You have one of the attributes of God engraved on each of these plaques. Then you hang the plaques up in your house in a conspicuous place where you have to pass by them every day. Each day as you pass them they remind you of the nature of God. Suppose that one day you start to go past those plaques, and you just reach up and take one of them down; perhaps you select the plaque that has "sovereignty" engraved on it, and you take it to the back room of your house and put it on a shelf in the closet. Then you walk back by those plaques and go to work, but you live that day as if God were not sovereign. That's practical atheism. You might encounter a problem that day, and you reason in your mind that it is of human origin; somebody did this, or somebody caused that. Or you might reason that it's happening by chance, that it is an accident. That's practical atheism. That's living as if God were not sovereign. I find in my own life that I have to be constantly reminded that God is sovereign, that He is in control, that He is good, that His goodness is absolute. **He does or permits nothing in my life but that which is in my best interest.**

There are many passages of Scripture that declare each of these two attributes of God, His sovereignty and His goodness. Let's look at a few of them, and let me suggest that you be especially on the lookout for the word *all*. My favorite passage as a text for this study is Romans 8:28.

• And we know that God causes all things to work together for good to them who love God, to those who are called according to His purpose [Rom. 8:28].

Notice how **sovereignty** and **goodness** are coupled together in this verse. Note that there are two things that Romans 8:28 does **not** say that we need to be clear on if we're going to interpret the verse correctly. First, Romans 8:28 does **not** say that **all things are good**. It says that God causes all things to **work together for good**, which is quite different. There are bad things that come into our lives, but God works those along with all other things for our ultimate good. Second, Romans 8:28 does **not** say or imply that God **causes** sin. Scripture is clear on this, especially the book of James (see James 1:13ff), but many other places as well. God is **not** the cause of sin. **We** are the cause of sin by our own choices. God **is,** however, the cause of the **effects** of sin in any life and in any situation. In other words the sins, though they are bad, are part of the all things that He works together for good.

Now notice in Romans 8:28 the word *all*. God causes **all** things. Now, dear friends, you and I must decide what "all" means in this verse. Of course, we know the definition of the word *all*. But we don't always act as if "all" means "all" in Romans 8:28, do we? And if "all" means "all" in Romans 8:28, then there is **no such thing** as chance, or an accident. To the world, things sometimes look like accidents or chance. I would admit that the idea of an accident might be a useful concept for the world. They use it in insurance. They use it in determining liability, and other things. But for a believer in Christ, it is not a valid concept at all. The Scriptures make that clear, especially Romans 8:28.

Here is a verse from the book of Proverbs.

• The lot is cast into the lap, but its every decision is from the Lord [Prov. 16:33].

If we were writing this verse today, we might say, "The dice are thrown, but God determines how they come up." He is in control of the outcome. In this verse the word "all" is *every*, meaning the same thing. **Every** decision is from God. There is no such thing as chance.

To me, one of the most remarkable verses in the entire Bible is Psalm 139:16. Here's what it says. David is speaking to God.

• Your eyes saw my unformed body. All the days ordained for me were in your book before one of them came to be [Psa. 139:16 (NIV)].

This is one of the verses in the Bible that teaches predestination, or *predeterminism*. I do not understand this very well. I do not understand how the free choice of man interacts with the sovereignty of God, nevertheless Scripture teaches both. God created us in His image. Part of that image is the ability to reason and choose. I would certainly admit that our choice is not the same as God's. He's the Creator, and we are the creatures. Our choice is limited. It has boundaries on it. But within those boundaries, we are free. And what is important for us to understand in connection with this study is that we are free to sin, or free to obey. That I believe is what Scripture teaches. I believe that God in His foreknowledge knew every decision that I would ever make in my life, both sins and obedience. God knew every decision every person who would touch my life would make. And He wove all of it together into a detailed plan, spoken of in this verse. Then He ordained that plan for me before I was ever born. We have an expression for it today. We would say, "It is chiseled in stone." And how much of my life was chiseled in stone before I was born? Well, the verse says "all." "**All** the days ordained for me were in your book before one of them came to be." Do I understand that? No, I don't. But I believe it. And if I am interpreting it correctly, it has profound application for our daily lives.

One of the great application verses for what we're discussing here is in the book of First Thessalonians.

• Be joyful always. Pray continually. Give thanks in all circumstances, for this is the will of God for you in Christ Jesus [1 Thess. 5:16-18 (NIV)].

This study has given new meaning to that passage to me. If *Square One* is not true, then this passage makes no sense whatever. It's a cruel joke for God to command us to give thanks in all circumstances, if our premise is not true. But if God is in control and has our best interest at heart, then not only does this passage make sense, but it's also a sin not to obey it. I believe that all means *all* in this verse. Give thanks in *all* circumstances.

From our class study came some very penetrating questions that we must ask ourselves: "when trouble and heartache and pain come, ask yourself, do I understand that this pain had its origin in God? And do I understand that the people involved are **merely God's agents?** And do I believe that this is **for my good**?" These three questions are penetrating ones. We can go in all kinds of directions with them. This applies to **everything**, good times, hard times, tragedy, suffering, conflict.

I want to key on the second of the three questions for the remainder of this study. Here is the question; "When trouble, heartache and pain come, do I understand that the people involved are merely God's agents?" Would you agree with me today that except for a major tragedy, most of the time when there is trouble and heartache and pain, it involves another person or persons? I think most would agree with that. I personally believe that the most important application of *Square One*, outside of tragedy or extreme suffering, is to *interpersonal relationships*.

The Bible has much to say on this subject. How do sovereignty and goodness apply to *interpersonal relationships*? The next statement that I am going to make is going to shock some of you. It shocked me the first time I heard it. Some of you will accept it as truth.   Some of you may reject it immediately.   Some of you will take it in and put it on probation and meditate on it for the next few hours or days, and come to your own conclusion. That's what I hope you will do. Don't accept it; don't reject it; but take it in and meditate on it if you have trouble accepting it. Here is the statement as it came to me from the teacher of our businessmen's class years ago: **"If you truly believe that God is in control and has your best interest at heart, then Biblically there is *no such thing* as a problem with another person."** Meditate on that for a moment. When I heard that for the first time there was an initial shock and rejection from my heart, but within 30 seconds after I heard it, I knew it was true. This is not saying that a problem does not exist; rather it is saying the problem is intrinsically and fundamentally with God, not the other person. This is an application of the truth that I have largely missed during most of my Christian life. And my life changed at that instant, and has never been the same since. I have spent many hours in recent years meditating on this truth, and searching the Scripture, and my conviction grows stronger by the day that it is in fact the truth.

I don't want to just give you this statement and leave it hanging. Here is a verse that I think teaches the truth contained in the statement, "there is no such thing as a problem with another person."

• So we say with confidence, the Lord is my helper, I will not be afraid. What can man do to me? [Heb. 13:6 (NIV)].

The last phrase of that verse is a rhetorical question that solicits a negative answer by implication. Let me state the verse again and supply the implied answer. "So we say with confidence, the Lord is my helper, I will not be afraid. *What can man do to me?*" The implied answer, *nothing without God's permission.* That's the gist of it. Every believer in Christ must face this question, "To what extent can another person influence my life without God's permission?" You must answer that for yourself. I believe that Scripture teaches that the answer is, "To *no* extent can another person influence my life **without God's permission**." That being true, then my problem is never with another person, **my problem is with God**, and the other person in my life is **God's agent** placed in my life for **God's purposes**, to participate in **God's plan** for my life. To be sure, other people can and will sin against me, but when they do, they are simply participating negatively in God's plan for my life; they do not alter my destiny. People who sin against me will face the consequences of those sins, but God will use them in my life for my good, and they will **not alter my destiny.**[1]

There are seven conclusions that I believe are supported by Scripture relating to the application of *Square One* to interpersonal relationships. Let me prepare you in advance to receive these by saying that they are difficult to accept, and even more difficult to apply to daily life. Please understand that I am not trying to convince you that they are true. I only ask you to face the issues involved, to meditate, pray and search the Scriptures for yourself. Of all the doctrines I have been taught since I became a Christian, this one has made the most dramatic change to my life:

☐ If you feel that you have a problem with another person, it is a sign that you **do not understand God,** because other people who impact your life are **God's agents** programmed into your life to mold you into the life plan that God ordained for you in eternity past (see Psalm 139:16).

☐ Other people can and will sin against me, but when they do they merely participate negatively in God's plan for my life. They will face the consequences of their sins, but they will

---

1   God's Word tells us to overlook most sins (Prov. 19:11, 1 Pet. 4:8). The perspective in this essay might enable one to "cover" even more sins that would otherwise seem to be great wrongs. Also, we must never seek personal revenge (Matt. 5:44, Rom. 12:19-20, Prov. 20:22; 24-29).

The Bible does allow private discussion or even serious church discipline in efforts to restore a relationship after a serious sin (Matt. 18:15-17) that we cannot in good conscience simply ignore. But God tells us to act quickly to prevent bitterness (Eph. 4:26-27).   God also gives the government the authority to punish sins that are crimes (Rom. 13:1-4). If the offender will not reconcile, or the state cannot enforce justice, then eventually we must leave the matter with God. Whether we choose to overlook another's sin or go in private for reconciliation, at some point everyone who has been wronged should forgive (see pp. 30-32, 45-49).

not alter my destiny. **God will not delegate my destiny to any person or force in the universe**.

☐ If God can act only in my best interest, and if He will not let anyone else act contrary to my best interest, then I am forced to the conclusion that **I alone** can hurt or destroy my life, and I do that by sin and disobedience. But whatever God does will be for my good (see Romans 8:28 and Hebrews 13:6).

☐ Since my fundamental problem is not with other people, I should always take my complaint to God not *primarily* to people (See footnote 1, above). Complaints are not always wrong; rebellion is **always** wrong. If I complain to God, not in a spirit of rebellion, retaining my worship and obedience to Him, He will hear me with an understanding, sympathetic, loving ear. This is not a problem for God. I can even get angry with God as long as I don't rebel or threaten Him. The great illustration of this is the patriarch Job. Job got angry with God. He took his complaint to God and God heard him. Jesus did so when He pleaded: "My God, my God, why hast thou forsaken me?" (Matt. 27:46, see also Lam. 1:21-22).

☐ For a believer in Christ, there is no such thing as being a victim. If I am harboring a victim mentality, then I am engaging in practical atheism, as Dr. Spurgeon taught. There is nothing happening to me that God has not ordained. He's working all things together for my good.

☐ The application of *Square One* to daily life is the path to peace with all people. It is the answer to interpersonal relationship problems.

☐ Holding all the Scripture passages included in this study together and in focus, the thesis of this essay can be summarized in one simple statement: **No matter what happens to me, and no matter who touches my life, it is with God's permission, under His control, and with my best interest in His heart.** And one day, when I step into eternity, and faith becomes sight, I will not regret a single circumstance of my life. My only regret will be my own disobedience and lack of faith.

Endorsements

"Dr. Steven Waterhouse in his book *Life's Tough Questions* has courageously and compassionately addressed crucial life issues and situations that many Christians find themselves enduring. Dr. Waterhouse has integrated his extensive pastoral experience, pastoral counseling background and a thorough study of Scripture to offer an insightful book that will assist both Christian people and Christian leaders. Dr. Waterhouse has obviously wrestled deeply with the many facets of human pain and suffering and his book addresses crucial topics that will equip people who are called by God to care for others whether it is in pastoral or counseling ministry. This book should be part of every pastor's library." **Dr. Alan Meenan, Senior Pastor, Hollywood Presbyterian Church, Hollywood, CA.**

"I highly recommend *Life's Tough Questions* by Dr. Steven Waterhouse. Today's life seems tougher than ever. New technology is ongoing, and with it comes difficult ethical decisions. Also, each year, our clinics treat a greater number of people just trying to deal with day-to-day stresses. Dr. Waterhouse's advice is timely and right on target." **Paul Meier, M.D., Founder of Meier Clinics**

Endorsements, Continued

"Based solidly on the Bible, *Life's Tough Questions* strikes a balanced and practical position for those who want to be guided by Biblical principles and counsel. In one helpful chapter, Waterhouse summarizes the Biblical information concerning mental illness and demon possession and suggests guidelines to delineate between the two. The chapter about suffering is an excellent review of the divine perspective and the human issues. For the layman who wants to understand better the agonies faced by the mentally ill, Waterhouse writes compassionately and insightfully about this traumatic disease. I recommend that pastors, counselors, and seminarians add *Life's Tough Questions* to their set of often-used reference books." **Dr. Vernon Sivage, Academic Dean, Uganda Baptist Seminary**

"Dr. Steve Waterhouse courageously tackles a number of very complex, thorny issues, displaying a nice balance of theological sophistication, solid psychological principles and common sense. He honors the absolute truth of biblical authority while respecting other viewpoints within the community of Christian orthodoxy. He speaks not only as a seasoned clergyman but with the credibility of personal life and family experiences, especially with respect to mental illness issues." **Phil Swihart, Ph.D., Clinical Psychologist and Director, Counseling Services, Focus on the Family**

ADDITIONAL SOURCES FOR
ASSISTANCE

Care Net
109 Carpenter Drive, Suite 110
Sterling VA 20164
(703) 478-5661

Focus on the Family
9605 Explorer Drive
Colorado Springs CO 80920
(719) 531-3400

**NAMI (National Alliance for the
Mentally Ill)**
2107 Wilson Boulevard, Suite 300
Arlington VA 22201
(703) 524-7600

Paul Meier Clinics
2099 North Collins Boulevard, Suite 100
Richardson TX 75080
(972) 437-4698